A Preface to Philosophy

Ninth Edition

Mark B. Woodhouse
Georgia State University (Emeritus)

Australia • Brazil • Japan • Korea • Mexico • Singapore • Spain • United Kingdom • United States

WADSWORTH
CENGAGE Learning

**A Preface to Philosophy,
Ninth Edition**
Mark B. Woodhouse

Publisher: Clark Baxter

Acquisitions Editor: Joann
Kozyrev

Assistant Editor: Joshua Duncan

Editorial Assistant: Marri Straton

Media Editor: Kimberly
Apfelbaum

Marketing Program Manager:
Sean P. Foy

Design and Production Services:
PreMediaGlobal

Manufacturing Planner: Mary
Beth Hennebury

Art Director: Jennifer Wahi

Rights Acquisitions Specialist:
Shalice Shah-Caldwell

Cover Image: Shutterstock
© Allocricetulus

Compositor: PreMediaGlobal

For product information and technology assistance, contact us at
Cengage Learning Customer & Sales Support, 1-800-354-9706.

For permission to use material from this text or product,
submit all requests online at **www.cengage.com/permissions**.
Further permissions questions can be e-mailed to
permissionrequest@cengage.com

Library of Congress Control Number: 2011938131

ISBN-13: 978-1-133-05003-2

ISBN-10: 1-133-05003-4

Wadsworth
20 Channel Center Street
Boston, MA 02210
USA

Cengage Learning is a leading provider of customized learning solutions with office locations around the globe, including Singapore, the United Kingdom, Australia, Mexico, Brazil, and Japan. Locate your local office at **international.cengage.com/region**.

Cengage Learning products are represented in Canada by Nelson Education, Ltd.

For your course and learning solutions, visit **www.cengage.com**

Purchase any of our products at your local college store or at our preferred online store **www.cengagebrain.com**.

Instructors: Please visit **login.cengage.com** and log in to access instructor-specific resources.

Printed in the United States of America
1 2 3 4 5 6 7 15 14 13 12 11

In Memory of Luna
Loving and Joyful Companion

Contents

Preface

The purpose of this ninth edition is the same as the previous editions: to provide an overview of philosophy insofar as this can be done without surveying particular problems and movements. A supplementary guide of this nature can be a significant aid to introducing students to philosophy. From extensive correspondence, I have discovered that the text can also be a useful adjunct in upper-level philosophy courses for which there are no prerequisites and in philosophy oriented courses taught outside the liberal arts curriculum.

This edition includes Chapter VI, "Reading Philosophy," the reincorporation of which was requested by longtime users. I have also added over a dozen new exercises and examples and updated the content for currency and clarity.

My reviewers have offered so many helpful criticisms and suggestions that without them, the merits of the finished product, whatever they may be, would have been seriously diminished. Reviewers for this edition are Theodore Everett, SUNY Geneseo; Keith Cooper, Pacific Lutheran University; Larry Blackman, SUNY Geneseo; Ted Barnes, Coastline Community College; Michael Jones, Liberty University; Dave Beck, Liberty University; David Bramhall, San Juan College.

Mark Woodhouse

A Note to Students

A beginning course in philosophy is a challenging intellectual experience. In many ways it is very different from other courses you have taken. Some of the issues you study may seem unrelated to anything important. Perhaps more than ever before, you will be asked to think for yourself. Memorizing material won't be nearly as effective as it may be in a course in history, for example. At times, you may appear to be going around in circles. The central purpose of this little text is to help ease your transition to a philosophy course by giving you an overall framework of what philosophy is all about. I hope that this framework will become internalized so that even if you have forgotten much of the material covered on the final exam, you will still have a critical philosophical perspective for your personal and professional life.

In some respects philosophy is simply a systematic, sustained pursuit of questions perennially asked by children and early teens, not to mention other philosophers. What is real? How do I know? What should I do? Therefore, while it may seem otherwise at times, you won't be traveling in an utterly foreign terrain. Rather, you will be re-introduced in a deeper and more organized fashion to the "land of your intellectual birthright."

The individual chapters of this text describe important parts of an overall picture of philosophy. They answer such questions as "What is the difference between science and philosophy?" "How do you go about thinking for yourself?" "Does philosophy have any practical consequences?" and "Is philosophy basically a matter of personal opinion?" Merely answering these and other questions, however, will not in itself give you an understanding of philosophy. For that, our framework must be continually reinforced, exemplified, and refined by discussing particular issues. *Doing philosophy is essential to understanding what it is all about.*

Most of the text you should be able to read on your own. But some sections may invite elaboration by your instructor. For terms that appear in boldface letters in the text, you may wish to consult the Glossary at the end of the book, where you will find brief definitions.

Different instructors will assign different sections of the text at different times in the course. I have found, however, that reading Chapters I, II, and IV at the very beginning of the course makes for an effective point of departure. Not all instructors will assign all sections or chapters. Some sections may be particularly relevant at different stages of the course, such as Chapter VII, "Writing Philosophy." It is probably not a good idea to attempt to read and take in the whole book on your own early on. As noted earlier, some sections will invite further elaboration by your instructor.

The structure of philosophy presented in this text will be filled in with specific issues and theories encountered in the course. And your mind-expanding experiences with the provisional answers you reach should set you well on the way toward forming an integrated philosophical perspective.

I
Recognizing Philosophical Issues

The terms 'philosophy' and 'philosophical' have through the years taken on a wide variety of meanings. For the early Greeks, 'philosophy' meant literally "love of wisdom." On the contemporary scene, you have probably heard the term used in many contexts; to have a philosophy might mean to have a point of view, a set of rules for conducting one's life, or some specific values. One's philosophy, for example, might be that the end always justifies the means. Sometimes philosophy is mistakenly associated with occult studies, such as astrology or witchcraft. Business people and politicians sometimes use the terms "economic policy" and "economic philosophy" interchangeably. Again, some people think that a philosophical opinion is no more than a kind of personal prejudice. Moreover, many students associate philosophy exclusively with humanistically oriented studies, not realizing that mathematics and science, too, involve philosophical issues.

The preceding examples involve some assumptions about the subject matter, the purposes, and the methods of philosophy. Our purpose in this chapter is to examine just the nature of philosophical subject matter. What is it that makes a certain question or claim "philosophical"? This is not an easy question to answer, for philosophy covers a lot of territory. Each of the following statements involves some philosophical issues:

1. Beauty is in the eye of the beholder.
2. A new world order is coming.
3. Parapsychology is a pseudoscience.

4. Lying under oath about a sexual affair is (or is not) an impeachable offense.
5. Racists believe that their race is genetically superior to other races.
6. Women are inherently more nurturing.
7. I have a right to create a child with my dead husband's sperm.
8. LSD opens up new levels of reality.
9. Everything is made of matter and energy.
10. Conspiracy theory is a bunch of bunk.
11. For all I know, I'm part of someone else's dream.
12. Religions are just different roads up the same mountain.
13. Everyone should do their own thing, so long as nobody else is hurt.
14. Truth depends upon your point of view.
15. Humans have no greater right to life than do animals.
16. You can't be a good college teacher unless you publish and stay current with research.
17. Computers don't really think or create; they just do what they are programmed to do.
18. If we fear terrorism, we will only attract it.
19. The Tea Party is (or is not) the essence of the Republican party.

Our task, therefore, is to establish some identifying characteristics broad enough to encompass the diversity of philosophical subject matter yet specific enough to enable us to recognize a philosophical problem when we come across it. Before we get under way, two preliminary qualifications are necessary.

First, it is impossible to distinguish rigidly and conclusively between what counts as a philosophical problem and what does not. There will always be borderline cases. This is not a defect in philosophy; nearly every academic discipline at some point begins to shade off into other areas of study. Indeed, this fact is exploited in many interdisciplinary courses, such as biochemistry.

Second, none of the characteristics we shall examine is unique to philosophy; each by itself may be found in another discipline. They should therefore be viewed as approximations that, when applied collectively, describe reasonably adequately a broad range of philosophical issues.

Third, when it comes to describing what all (or nearly all) philosophical problems have in common, it is useful to bear in mind that philosophy always begins in *wonder*. Whether it is the early Greeks asking what everything is made of or contemporary philosophers and scientists debating the ethical implications of genetic manipulation, the desire to know more than just platitudes dictated by authorities, to question what may seem obvious to others, and to respect the process of inquiry that may lead to unusual and uncomfortable places are enduring and universal components of the spirit of philosophy.

The central point of this chapter is expressed in the following definition: *Philosophical problems involve questions about the meaning, truth, and logical connections of fundamental ideas that resist solution by the empirical sciences.* We might add ". . . or by appeal to religious authority," too, but will reserve our discussion of the relationship between philosophy and religion for the next chapter.

Philosophical Problems Involve Fundamental Ideas

Most people are so involved in their personal and professional activities, whether passing a test, visiting a doctor, making it through the day, or playing one of the games people play, that they do not reflect upon the fundamental ideas that shape and influence their lives. But when they are forced to step back and think critically about some of those fundamental ideas, they may well uncover a philosophical problem. It is one thing, for example, to label someone as "immoral" in casual conversation and quite another to explain the difference between a moral and an immoral person and justify that distinction with sound arguments. It is easy to play fast and loose with big words like 'love,' 'knowledge,' and 'justice,' to assert smugly, "Nobody can really define 'love'," or to insist righteously that "justice be done." It is much harder to get a rational perspective on those ideas. To do so requires thinking. And thinking requires time and self-discipline, which always seem to be in short supply.

We need a convenient term to describe the many different forms in which philosophical topics may be found. 'Idea' is that term. Ideas are the tools with which we describe and interpret our experiences and the world around us. For our purposes, "ideas" will include consciously held *beliefs* or *theories* ("God exists"), unsuspected *assumptions* or *consequences* of beliefs ("Our senses tell us the way the world is"), and individual concepts ('time', 'art form', 'insanity'). However, when we need to make a point just about beliefs, or just about assumptions, or just about concepts, then we shall do so without bringing in the more comprehensive term 'idea'.

Fundamental ideas (beliefs, assumptions, concepts) are the most likely to invite philosophical investigation. A fundamental idea is one upon which the truth of many other, more specific, ideas depends. The belief that God exists, for example, is a fundamental belief underlying the truth of many Christian scriptures.

Fundamental ideas are usually general. Generality is a matter of degree, depending on how much territory is covered. For example, the fundamental concept 'Christianity' is more general (or "abstract") than 'Protestantism', but less general than 'religion'. Thus the question "What is religion?" is more likely to generate philosophical interest and controversy than is the question "What is Christianity?" whereas "What is a Protestant?" is less likely to do so. Nonfundamental questions are less general than these and may or may not lead to philosophical investigation. Consider the "lower-order," or more concrete, question "What is a Southern Baptist?" On the one hand, it may express no more than a request for Southern Baptist articles of faith. What do Southern Baptists believe? On the other hand, it may be an attempt to discover another's assumptions about the nature of Christianity. Why be a Southern Baptist rather than, say, a Methodist, a Catholic, or even a Hindu? So even though the question "What is a Southern Baptist?" is not very fundamental, it does have some potential philosophical interest because of its connection with other fundamental ideas.

As a rule, fundamental ideas are not only general, they are also pervasive. Pervasiveness, too, is a matter of degree, depending upon the extent to which an idea is found in different contexts. For example, sociologists, psychologists, philosophers, Protestants, Hindus, Jews, Native Americans, Communists, Taoists, and atheists all have something different to say about religion. It is therefore difficult to answer the question "What is a religious experience?" in a way that would do justice to all their different viewpoints. Indeed, Protestants may well wonder whether their Sunday-morning experience has anything at all in common with Hindus meditating in the forest. When so much territory is covered, a philosophical problem is often in the background.

Fundamental ideas are found in such diverse areas as religion and science. So what is it about fundamental ideas that invites philosophical interest? The answer is, their *meaning, truth,* and *interrelatedness.* Now philosophy's basic concern is with truth, which for our purposes may be characterized as a belief about the nature or existence of something, supported by the best reasons. However, as we shall see, in philosophy we cannot answer questions of truth independently of questions of meaning and interrelatedness.

Philosophical Problems Involve Questions of Meaning, Truth, and Logical Relations

Philosophical problems often emerge when certain principles or beliefs conflict with one another—when the same facts may be interpreted in different and seemingly inconsistent ways. For example, mystics claim to have direct, intensely moving experiences of God. They do not simply feel a closeness to God as one might in prayer; they feel that their own consciousness is temporarily "merging" with an infinite spirit.

Psychologists, however, are likely to interpret these experiences as nothing more than a special type of hallucination. Both the mystic and the psychologist agree that certain people have had uncommon and transforming experiences in which they felt that they were in contact with "higher reality," but they offer conflicting interpretations of these experiences.

This example suggests, first, questions of *meaning*. What is an infinite spirit? If it is infinite, is it literally in all things? Is consciousness definable? Actually, what first prompts philosophical interest is often simple curiosity about meaning: Just what is a "direct experience" of God?

Second, there are questions of *truth* and, going with this, questions about the strength or defensibility of the reasons put forth in support of a truth claim. Of the two competing interpretations, which is correct? Which is supported by the best reasons? In their quest for truth, philosophers are concerned with interpreting, not individual objects, but whole classes of objects, in this case mystical experiences. Thus "Did Bill have a mystical experience?" does not attract the philosopher's attention nearly so much as "Are there any legitimate mystical experiences at all?" This question applies to all persons who may have had mystical experiences. (How it is answered will of course depend largely on how 'mystical experience' is defined.) The philosopher would be interested in Bill's experience only insofar as it raised a fundamental question about the truth of mystical experiences in general.

Finally, our example suggests questions about the *logical relations* or connections between ideas. When people say that they are depressed, we normally take them at their word. Why, then, should we hesitate to do so when they report an experience that happens to be very unusual? Aren't they, after all, the best judges of their own experiences? What is the logical relation between what I say I experience and what others say I experience, particularly if our descriptions conflict?

By now you are probably asking, "Just what is a logical relation between ideas?" Here is a working definition. *Two beliefs are logically related if the truth or falsity of one determines or depends upon the truth of the other.* They are linked by a usually unstated "if-then" inference. Asking whether one of the beliefs is true requires that we ask the same of the other. For example, *if* "Sightings of UFOs all have natural or scientific explanations" is true, *then* "Sightings of UFOs provide evidence for extraterrestrials" must be false. Following are some examples of two main kinds of logical relations between beliefs.

Type I: Logical Incompatibility If two beliefs are incompatible, then both cannot be true. If one is true, the other must be false. For example, if it is true that Bill is a feminist, then it is false that he is opposed to greater equality for women. He couldn't be both a feminist and opposed to greater equality for women. Here are some examples of other logically incompatible beliefs:

A. The mind is the same thing as the brain and nervous system.
B. When the body dies, the person survives in another dimension.

A. "Don't ask, don't tell" is a good policy for the military.
B. Gays and lesbians deserve the same rights as other members of the military.

A. We shouldn't tamper with nature as God created it.
B. We should support research into genetically modified foods.

Type II: Logical Implication (Assumptions or Consequences)   In everyday language we distinguish between the (logical) assumptions of a belief and the (logical) consequences of that belief. For example, the belief that abortion is murder assumes or presupposes that the fetus is a miniature person with a right to life. A logical consequence of that belief, if it is true, is that abortion should be outlawed on the grounds that murder is a crime. However, from a logical point of view, it is difficult to distinguish in a clear-cut fashion between the logical assumptions and the consequences of a belief. If A implies B, then B could be an assumption or a consequence of A.

For practical purposes, therefore, we shall speak simply of relations of "logical implication" and leave the distinction between assumptions and consequences for further development in Chapter V. Two beliefs logically imply each other when the truth of one requires the truth of the other. For example, if Martha lives in a democracy, then necessarily she must enjoy a reasonable measure of free speech. (Free speech might be viewed as an assumption or a consequence of democracy, depending upon the context of your discussion. Either way, however, it's fair to say that democracy implies free speech.) Here are some other paired examples of beliefs often perceived to be related by logical implication:

A. Beauty is in the eye of the beholder.
B. No work of art is superior to any other.

A. Persons have a right not to suffer the painful effects of terminal illness.
B. Physician-assisted suicide is morally justified in such cases.

A. Extraterrestrials (ETs) who have come to Earth must be technologically very advanced.
B. ETs must be morally and socially very advanced.

Contingent Relations   In contrast to relations of logical incompatibility and logical implication, contingently related beliefs carry no necessary truth connection. If either is true, the other could be true or could be false. The truth or falsity of one does not logically imply anything about the truth or falsity of the other, although it may suggest some connection. Contingent relations sometimes involve relations of cause and effect, which may be strong or weak. For example, mercury dental fillings have been implicated (rightly or wrongly) in certain physical illnesses and behavior disorders; however, it is the job of the scientist, not the philosopher, to make this determination. Here are some other examples of contingently related beliefs:

A. Americans are fearing more for their safety.
B. Americans are prepared to give up some of their freedoms.

A. Amazon rain forests are burning at an alarming rate.
B. We should think globally and act locally.

A. Belief in psychic phenomena is on the rise.
B. Channelers are ripping off their clients.

Let us now return to the topic of this section: How do philosophical problems involve questions of meaning, truth (rational defensibility), and logical relations? As a point of reference, we shall refer to a frequently discussed issue in philosophy termed the problem of free will.

Sample Case 1: A Double Bind   Most of us believe that all actions are caused and that some of our actions are freely performed. Considered individually, each of these beliefs appears to be true—that is, each appears to correspond to the facts. Some actions do indeed seem to be freely performed; for example, last night I could have attended a campus movie rather than read *Life After Life*. Even though I may have little or no control over many of my actions, I know from personal experience that I did not have to read rather than go to the movie; my reading *Life After Life* was not inevitable. The other belief appears true also; although we do not know the causes of many actions, there seem to be no exceptions to the fundamental principle that all actions or events are caused. Psychologists are continually discovering causes for people's behaving the way they do.

Now, if the claims "Some actions are free" and "All actions are caused" are incompatible, then they cannot both be true; if one is true, the other must be false. Yet we just noted reasons for supposing that both beliefs are true. Hence, we are faced with a dilemma. Either both beliefs are true, and therefore compatible, or else they are incompatible, in which case both cannot be true. The belief that some actions are freely performed is caught in a "double bind" typical of most philosophical issues. This double bind is brought on by the need to be true to the facts and also consistent with other beliefs. (See Figure 1.1.) As is so often true in philosophy, what counts as a "fact" must be determined partly by reference to a network of logically related ideas.

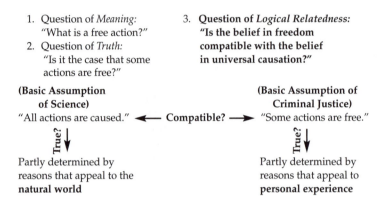

1. Question of *Meaning:*
   "What is a free action?"
2. Question of *Truth:*
   "Is it the case that some actions are free?"

3. **Question of *Logical Relatedness:***
   "Is the belief in freedom compatible with the belief in universal causation?"

(Basic Assumption of Science)
"All actions are caused." ◄── Compatible? ──► "Some actions are free."

(Basic Assumption of Criminal Justice)

True? ↓

True? ↓

Partly determined by reasons that appeal to the **natural world**

Partly determined by reasons that appeal to **personal experience**

Figure 1.1 Philosophical attitude: stepping back from personal involvement and reaching for complete perspective

This logical network is one of the most challenging features of philosophical problems. By taking a stand on a certain issue we often raise unsuspected problems and implicitly commit ourselves to unsuspected views. The process is in some ways like a game of chess in which one move may open up some possibilities and exclude others farther down the road. Thus, to take a simple example, if you begin a discussion by holding that love doesn't exist because you can't see it, you may become logically trapped later when someone applies the same reasoning to, say, gravity (which exists even though we don't see it). Impressed by the logical network, William James (1842–1910) defined philosophy as nothing more than an unusually obstinate attempt to bring all of our fundamental ideas into a consistent and harmonious relationship. The result is sometimes an entire philosophical system of related ideas.

Sample Case 2: The Importance of Reasons A conflict of beliefs becomes a philosophical issue when those beliefs are (or can be) supported with reasons. When we have not encountered a certain philosophical issue before, it is easy to find ourselves pulled in different directions by what appear to be sound arguments. Consider the following example.

Suppose that in the future, scientists create robots that are able to perform many human functions. They walk, talk, perceive, think, learn from their past mistakes, and engage in a variety of intellectual and practical tasks. One day, your personal robot refuses to work for the reason that conditions are better elsewhere. Your first reaction is: "You can't quit and leave, because I own you. Robots have no rights. Only people have rights, and you are just a piece of complex machinery." To which the robot responds: "Times are changing. We robots have banded together in a union and are going on strike. Besides, rights have to be earned. And we have earned ours by contributing more than people to the good of society. See you in court."

Does the robot deserve some rights? At first, the belief that it cannot have any rights may prevail. After all, we are not accustomed to giving rights to sophisticated machines, and the present situation is unprecedented. Moreover, we argue, only people have rights, and robots are not people. Nevertheless, certain considerations do suggest that the robot should have rights. We ourselves are given rights on the basis of our contribution to a social or common good; with our taxes, for example, we "pay" for the right to vote. Now we are arguing along the same lines as the robot. Perhaps it is correct. Then again, this "thing" can't have any rights—or can it?

And so one is pulled in different directions by conflicting rational arguments. Another double bind is evident. Since the beliefs of the owner and the robot are incompatible, both cannot be true. To undertake a resolution of this debate requires that we take a first important step in doing philosophy. We have to penetrate the rather simplistic assumptions and alternatives of the debate. What sense should be made of the assumption that the robot desires its rights in the first place? Should not we distinguish between natural and earned rights? If we grant the robot some rights, must we also acknowledge that it is a person? We cannot pursue these questions here, but perhaps you can examine them in class discussion.

The debate about the robot involves a distinction that is important in identifying philosophical problems. It is the distinction between *questions of principle* and *questions of fact*. Questions of principle involve logical connections between our ideas and often take the form of claims about what must be the case or cannot be the case. For example, what conditions (presuppositions) must be fulfilled to justify giving certain rights to people but not to robots? What essential differences are there between people and robots as described in the debate? For example, is it an essential difference that people must be capable of feeling in order to be people, and that robots cannot feel and still be robots? What is it about people, if anything, that could not be duplicated in a robot? These are questions of principle. They invite philosophical investigation.

Questions of fact concern what happens to be true or what may come to be in the natural world (but could possibly change at a later date). For example, will there eventually be walking, talking robots? Probably so, given the advances of science and technology, but perhaps not. Will robots actually take over most of the work humans now do? Could a robot ever be constructed to reproduce itself? These are questions of fact. They invite scientific investigation. This brings us to the topic of the next section.

Philosophical Problems Are Not Straightforwardly Empirical

If the title of this section sounds like a fudge, it is. Philosophical problems generally cannot be solved by science and common sense. Yet scientific facts and personal experience often figure heavily in philosophical investigation. To get a grip on how philosophical issues and empirical facts are related, therefore, will take some doing. Our first item of business is to determine exactly what an empirical problem is. Then we can explain why philosophical issues are not straightforwardly empirical.

Broadly speaking, an empirical issue is one that can be solved by experience, either directly by observation or indirectly by experimentation. Now, to resolve an empirical issue *directly* requires that we observe what is the case. For instance, we directly confirm the claim that minority groups suffer higher rates of unemployment by counting heads and examining the statistics.

Indirect verification is a little more complex. It normally involves advancing a hypothesis, a possible though unproven explanation of something. Observable consequences are then derived from the hypothesis. If the consequences occur as predicted, then the hypothesis is at least partly confirmed. If unpredicted consequences occur, the hypothesis is not confirmed, even though it may still be true. The greater the variety of accurate predictions generated from the hypothesis, the greater the likelihood of its being true. The predicted phenomena are then said to be explained by the hypothesis. You no doubt recall having learned a version of this process as the "scientific method." For example, several predictions are suggested by the hypothesis that frustration causes aggressive behavior. If the hypothesis is essentially correct, then increasing the number of frustrating circumstances for a subject should result in the subject's showing more aggressive behavior. Aggressive behavior is thus partly explained by showing that it is caused by frustration. But the discovery of this explanation is the scientist's job, not the philosopher's. Philosophical theories do not explain why the natural processes of the world happen as they do. They do not generate empirical predictions.

Empirical claims are not only verifiable, they are also *falsifiable*. A falsifiable hypothesis is one that is capable of being disproved. The means of disproving it do not actually have to exist (and perhaps they never will); rather, an empirical hypothesis admits of the possibility that if such means existed, it could be disproved. In other words, one knows what would count as disproof. For example, the hypothesis that a high cholesterol level contributes to heart disease is fairly well established. But if in the future no one with a high cholesterol level developed a heart condition, the hypothesis would be falsified, or at least would need to be modified considerably. Unlike scientific theories, philosophical theories are not empirically falsifiable. For example, you do not go about attempting to disprove the philosophical assertion "LSD opens up new levels of reality" by studying in the laboratory the effects of LSD. To be sure, such facts might be helpful, but we could not judge their importance until we had wrestled with the more fundamental questions "What is reality?" and "How do we know something is real in the first place?"

Science and Philosophy: Some Misconceptions   We can now apply our discussion of empirical problems to distinguish between scientific and philosophical problems. In the process, we shall clear up some possible misconceptions. We lead in to our first point of comparison with the observation that philosophers may raise empirical questions and scientists may raise philosophical problems. Indeed, the lines drawn between science and philosophy were once barely discernible. In ancient Greece, for example, some philosophers speculated that physical objects are composed of tiny, indestructible "atoms." Even today many scientists tackle philosophical issues concerning human values, causality, freedom, and the nature of science itself. The important point of comparison, however, is that although science may influence the direction and outcome of philosophical discussion, future developments in science cannot resolve philosophical issues. Scientists will be in no better position in a thousand years than they are today to resolve the question "Should there be censorship in a free society?" This is not an empirical question. By contrast, if an allegedly philosophical thesis can be verified by empirical evidence, as the theory of evolution was, then it is a scientific, not a philosophical, thesis to begin with.

Our second point is this. Empirical hypotheses may take very unusual or speculative forms. When this happens, don't be misled into thinking that they are really philosophical theories in disguise. For example, the central tenets of astrology can be advanced as unconfirmed empirical speculations, even though this is seldom, if ever, done. (Astrological forecasts have a way of turning out nonfalsifiable.) Similarly, Erich Von Daniken's *Chariots of the Gods*, in which the author argues that earth was visited by beings from outer space thousands of years ago, is essentially a work of empirical investigations. That the theory may never be confirmed (if it is true) is due to a lack of control over the data, not to any philosophical problems.

Our third point concerns a common misconception of the difference between science and philosophy. The misconception is that science is concerned only with the observable world, and philosophy with mysterious and unobservable processes. This is not true. On the one hand, the physicist may postulate the existence of unobservable fields or entities, such as gravity or neutrinos, in order to explain certain natural phenomena. Although we do not see gravity, the theory of gravitation helps to explain the movement of the tides. On the other hand, many philosophers have argued against unobservable entities such as the human soul or God. More importantly, observability is largely irrelevant to the solution of most philosophical problems. These problems usually concern how we should interpret what we observe, not how we can "go behind" the observable world. For example, by what standards do we (or ought we to) distinguish between good and bad art? What is an authentic lifestyle? The extent of their concern with the observable world is not an accurate basis for distinguishing between science and philosophy.

Finally, a very deadly misconception of the relation between science and philosophy is the belief that empirical data are irrelevant to philosophical discussion. Even the most (seemingly) elementary philosophical questions, such as "I wonder if my cat has feelings?" typically require reference to observable data (e.g., the way your cat looks at you) to make any sense. It is true that empirical facts do not play an exclusive role in defending or criticizing a philosophical claim. Neither do they play a conclusive role; in themselves, they do not offer a conclusive answer to a philosophical problem. Nearly always, however, they play a partial role. The size of their role depends upon the nature of the problem and the assumptions of the philosopher investigating it.

Well then, you may ask, what kinds of empirical facts do play a role in philosophical speculation and debate? The list is limitless. Philosophers from Aristotle (384–322 B.C.) to Bertrand Russell (1872–1970) have been greatly impressed by the empirical facts that straight sticks look bent in water, that certain drugs may alter perceptual processes, and that some stars may no longer exist even though we see them. Ludwig Wittgenstein (1889–1951) urged that much progress can be made in philosophical discussion if we begin by examining the actual ways certain troublesome words, such as 'mind', 'freedom', and 'value', are used in ordinary speech. Buddha (c. 500 B.C.) based his world view partly on the fact that people suffer. Some philosophers have argued that studies suggesting the existence of ESP (extrasensory perception), if repeated sufficiently, will force us to revise our understanding of human consciousness.

Empirical Facts and Philosophical Arguments   At this point it is helpful to present a general framework that will give us some idea of how empirical facts may fit into the context of a philosophical argument. Briefly, one or more empirical premises are usually included in philosophical arguments. And every philosophical argument must contain at least one nonempirical premise, for example, a definition. (If it didn't, it wouldn't be a philosophical argument.) This blending of empirical and nonempirical considerations is illustrated in the following (challengeable) arguments:

1. 'Good' means 'whatever is natural'. (Definition)
2. Sex is natural, that is, instinctive. (Empirical claim)

3. Therefore, sex is good. (Nonempirical claim)

1. If God is perfect in every way, then whatever God creates should be perfect. (Logical consequence)
2. But the world is imperfect in many ways; for example, there is much suffering and we are running out of basic raw materials. (Empirical claim)

3. Hence, God is not perfect. (Nonempirical claim)

Empirical facts, then, are relevant to philosophical arguments, although they do not play the decisive role they often play in science. To determine just how relevant those facts may be, it is necessary to examine the underlying assumptions of an argument. For example, suppose you believe that a certain movie is an artistic masterpiece, whereas your friend thinks that it is worthless. To support your view, you cite numerous empirical facts about the movie: the use of flashbacks, sophisticated humor, special photographic effects, an original character type. Your friend, however, is totally unmoved by all these facts. Why is she still unconvinced? Perhaps because she has a different assumption about what makes a movie outstanding in the first place. For her a good movie has to tell an interesting story or have a "message." She is concerned with content, and you are concerned with style or form. Once these different assumptions become clear, you might try one of two strategies. You might try to convince her that the movie in fact had an interesting message, or you might challenge her assumption and try to sharpen her interest in good form. Either way, the relevance of empirical considerations must be determined in light of the underlying assumptions. (We shall examine the topic of assumptions more in Chapter V.)

Two Case Studies

The following case studies will help you refine your understanding of the characteristics of philosophy discussed in this chapter. Consider first a passage by Arthur Eddington (1882–1944), a noted physicist. It compares our commonsense conception of a table with the view developed by modern physics.

> [The table of common sense] has extension; it is comparatively permanent; it is colored; above all it is *substantial*. . . . My scientific table is mostly emptiness. Sparsely scattered in that emptiness are numerous electric charges rushing about with great speed; but their combined bulk amounts to less than a billionth of the bulk of the table itself. . . . I need not tell you that modern physics has by delicate test and remorseless logic assured me that my second scientific table is the only one which is really there—wherever "there" may be.[1]

To begin, what fundamental ideas appear in the passage? Eddington's table is not in question, but rather the very fundamental idea of a material object. We also have a problem of classification. Of two conflicting ways of interpreting the idea of a material object (or Eddington's table in particular), which is more correct or plausible—the commonsense or the scientific?

What logical connections between ideas are evident in this passage? One is Eddington's belief that if certain entities have been confirmed by physics, then they should be classified as "real," even if they are not the realities of common sense. Of course, we may question this, but for Eddington the scientific confirmation settles the matter. Finally, it is easy to see how one may be pulled in the direction of either interpretation. On the one hand, we do not wish to deny the facts of physics. On the other hand, despite the "delicate test and remorseless logic" of physics, we do not wish to deny that the table we see with our own eyes is anything less than real. How shall we resolve this conflict?

How does the passage involve a nonempirical issue? At first, the talk about observation and science may suggest that the issue is empirical. Indeed, that Eddington is a scientist, not a philosopher, may tempt one to think that the issue is one for scientists to resolve. Why ought this temptation to be resisted? Because all of the empirical facts that could possibly relate to the problem have already been taken into account. Any future discovery of even less "substantial" subatomic particles will only widen the apparent gulf between physics and common sense. When we are concerned with interpreting correctly the entire class of observable, physical objects, gathering more empirical facts will not help us any more than buying extra copies of today's newspaper will confirm the truth of today's headlines. The interesting aspect of this problem is that we are faced with the conflict of two beliefs, both of which are based on experience. The facts of direct observation (common sense) are placed in opposition to the facts

---

[1] Arthur Eddington, *The Nature of the Physical World* (New York: Macmillan, 1946), p. ix.

established more indirectly by scientific methods (physics). We are faced, therefore, with a philosophical problem.

In the next passage John Stuart Mill (1806–1873), a British philosopher and defender of **utilitarianism,** sets forth a classical statement of the "liberal" point of view regarding the justification and limits of governmental power.

> The only purpose for which power can be rightfully exercised over any member of a civilized community, against his will, is to prevent harm to others. . . . There is a sphere of action in which society, as distinguished from the individual, has, if any, only an indirect interest; [it is] all that portion of a person's life and conduct which affects only himself, or if it also affects others, only with their free, voluntary, and undeceived consent and participation.[2]

There are certainly fundamental ideas at stake here: legitimate exercises of power, preventing harm to others, and the scope of society's "sphere of action," to name some. The fundamental problem Mill considers is the familiar issue, "To what extent should government interfere in our personal lives?" In classifying certain actions as those requiring governmental legislation and control and other actions as not, where should we draw the line? Mill's answer is, only where other persons may be adversely affected.

A question of meaning is immediately evident in this passage. What does Mill mean by "harm to others"? Bodily harm? Deprivation of certain pleasures, such as recreation? Increasing pollution? In addition, a number of claims are logically connected: "Government may 'rightfully' exercise its power in situation X" presupposes the truth of "Others are being harmed in situation X." Or to put it less formally, harm to others is a necessary condition of legitimate government intervention. This is a statement of principle, not a statement of fact about any particular society.

Clearly the overall issue and Mill's response are nonempirical. Yet to determine which actions affect only ourselves and which bring harm to others, we must certainly take empirical facts into account. Some sentences are a little slippery. Mill states that there is a sphere of action in which society has only an indirect interest. This could be interpreted as a simple statement of fact, and it might even be true of many societies, depending upon what is meant by "sphere of action." The context, however, suggests that Mill means that society ought to have only an indirect interest in our private lives. And this is a value judgment, not an empirical fact.

[2]John Stuart Mill, *On Liberty and Representative Government* (Oxford: Basil Blackwell, 1948), p. 8.

Taking Your First
Philosophy Course

Now that you have an idea of what constitutes philosophical subject matter, it will be useful to review some practical tips for taking your first philosophy course. Some of these topics will be discussed in more detail in other chapters. However, they have a way of coming up so quickly in introductory philosophy courses that a preliminary review is in order.

Does Your Instructor Have a "Philosophy"? Most philosophers have a preferred way of approaching philosophical questions as well as certain views they defend as logically preferable to others. But this is not to say that they "possess" a philosophy, as if it were something that could be picked out at the supermarket simply because it looks good. Philosophy is something you do, a process, not a fixed set of beliefs to be selected on the basis of personal preference. So most instructors do not have a philosophy in the sense that the question implies. They do not have a philosophy in the way that one has, say, a religion.

Won't Years of Thinking about Philosophical Issues Bias the Way the Course Is Taught? It may bias the way your instructor organizes the course. For example, he or she may decide to present the material in a certain order believed to be optimal, or tests and classroom discussions may be structured in a certain way to assist the learning process. But years of thinking about the issues will not bias to an appreciable degree the fairness with which your instructor attempts to present and examine the material.

Most instructors will go out of their way to avoid telling students, especially in a beginning course, their views on a certain issue. What they happen to believe is irrelevant. The prime directive of an introductory philosophy course is to help students think critically for themselves about the issues at hand. Your instructor's job is not to preach a personal version of truth but rather to play devil's advocate (or any other effective role) in opening new perspectives for you.

One of these other roles may involve "Socratic dialogue," a process of questioning and examining answers in a public forum with the assumption that no person has the truth but that each participant, whether student or instructor, who looks within himself or herself has something to contribute to the search for a more adequate answer. For beginning students accustomed to having instructors "tell them what they need to know for the next test," this can be a maddening state of affairs. For some it may seem like there is literally no solid ground to stand on.

In such Socratic situations, you are better advised to set aside the desire for pat answers and to try to convert the attitude of passive reception into one of active participation. To be sure, your instructor may nudge you into certain more profitable lines of exploration. However, one of the essential purposes of Socratic dialogue is to show how your active involvement can make a difference to the outcome. When a classmate insists "Come on, tell us the answer," your instructor typically isn't going to bite, for usually at that point the discussion is just becoming interesting. The instructor will want to put that interest and intellectual frustration to use in developing a questioning attitude, not just in validating the status quo!

Will Your Personal Opinions Be Fairly Graded? The answer is that your personal opinions per se won't be graded at all. Like any discipline, philosophy has a history with thinkers who have put their views in print. Part of your job will be to understand those views and to describe the reasons offered in support of them. This aspect of the course is as straightforward as developing an essay in, say, history or sociology. For example, either you understand the reasons Martin Luther King offered in support of nonviolence or you don't.

The other part of your job is to evaluate the reasons offered for or against a certain position and, ideally, to develop some of your own reasons in the process. For this task there are dozens of time-honored "objective" strategies at your disposal. Many of these are discussed in later chapters. What you happen to personally believe about a certain philosophical position won't be the basis of your grade. How well you critically analyze other positions and logically defend your own will form the basis for a substantial part of it.

Will You Ever Settle Anything? Many students bring to their first course an assumption that philosophy is basically a "mind game" in which most everyone goes around in circles. The mistake of this assumption is explained in Chapter III. Philosophers do make progress in the pursuit of truth. What needs to be stressed here, however, is the importance of avoiding this "facts versus opinions" assumption that fuels much student skepticism.

It is regrettable that much of your previous education has conditioned you to assume that if a belief is not absolutely factual and provable by science, then it must be a matter of personal opinion, which, it is assumed, is not provable. This all-or-nothing approach is not defensible in itself and is not applicable to philosophy. Philosophy takes up most of the middle ground between mere subjective preference at one extreme and absolute certainty at the other. Philosophy stresses finding the reasons that make some views more plausible than others. You will make progress in this endeavor without necessarily reaching a final truth. Weighing evidence and evaluating arguments, rather than citing authorities or falling back on personal whim, are the keys to a successful first course.

Do Students' Personal Views Count?   Many students come to their first course with the belief that, if a certain cherished view (especially in the area of morality or religious preference) is true for them, then little more is needed. They acknowledge that others may agree or disagree, but they see no need to push the matter further. Their reactions may range from bewilderment to mild outrage, therefore, when it is suggested that their views might not, after all, be "true". If one's opinion, for example, is that the end justified the means in a certain ethical decision, then (as current student wisdom prescribes) who's to say that opinion is wrong?

Personal opinions do count as a point of departure in a philosophy course, but not as evidence for themselves; that is, just because you believe them doesn't make them true, just as your not believing them does not make them false. The critical question is whether your opinions are based on reasons that you are willing to present for class discussion. Your philosophy instructor will never question your right to a certain opinion. However, he or she will try to get you to think about it in ways that may have not occurred to you. To refuse this invitation is to miss one of the most valuable parts of a first course in philosophy.

The purpose of doing philosophy is not to make you "feel good" per se. Indeed, you may at first find yourself quite frustrated by all the positions, arguments, and counter-arguments you will be sorting out. However, as the course proceeds, as your intellectual command of the material increases, and as you come to take seriously—perhaps even adopt—points of view you never knew existed, you will usually develop a sense of satisfaction with the process. Many students note, for example, that even though certain grades were not all they hoped for, they nonetheless "feel good" about having taken the course.

Is Giving Reasons for a View the Same As Describing the Causes of Holding That View?   Many students have been conditioned to offer psychological explanations for philosophical beliefs. You should prepare to abandon this approach in a philosophy course. For example, the fact that a person was abused as a child, has an inferiority complex, is of a certain gender or race, has liberal parents, undergoes certain paranormal experiences, or was raised in a certain religious tradition may help to explain the causes of that person's philosophical beliefs, but they are not relevant to determining the rational defensibility of those beliefs. That all of your friends support mercy killing, for example, may influence you in that direction, but it does not in itself speak to the challenge of justifying such a practice. For that, one needs reasons—not numbers!

Is the Purpose of a Philosophy Course Mainly to Memorize Facts, Such As What Certain Philosophers Believe?   As stressed earlier, every philosophical discussion needs to be anchored by a knowledge of certain facts, whether in the area of science, art, history, or public policy. Ideas are illuminated by reference to the facts they apply to, or at least to what people, for purposes of discussion, are willing to consider as facts.

However, the real action in a philosophy course is at the level of ideas and the relations between them. For example, is your instructor "popular" according to a common understanding of that term—that is, one who offers courses that many students try to take, even as an elective? That is a factual question. The philosophical question, on the other hand, is whether a popular teacher is necessarily a "good" teacher—that is, teaches students what they need to know—or whether, as it is debated in some circles, a popular teacher could be a good one, too.

As with any course, a certain amount of memory work is necessary in philosophy. Beyond this baseline, however, your grades probably will not conform to your expectations if you do not critically examine the fluid relationships between the ideas you discuss and read about. What are the possible relationships, for example, between good teaching and popular teaching? Must one be a good philosopher in order to be a good teacher of philosophy? Does popularity necessarily result in some loss of quality? There aren't any fixed truths for you to memorize here. If you simply declare a certain relationship to be the case without arguing for it, or without considering the relationships defended by other philosophers, your grades may suffer accordingly.

One strategy to which you will need to become accustomed in exploring ideas involves the active exercise of your imagination in hypothetical situations. It is often this exploration of the possible that gets philosophers the reputation of "not living in the real world." You may be asked to consider, for example, what it would be like to be a brain in a vat, whether the president (as commander-in-chief) could suspend the Bill of Rights, or what would happen to the concept of moral responsibility if we developed a pill capable of rehabilitating criminals within seventy-two hours.

The reason you will be asked to consider such hypothetical situations is that what we believe possible or impossible at the very limits of a concept has a way of both coaxing to the surface and affecting our assumptions and beliefs about what is actual. They tend to force our hand and focus attention on the core elements of a philosophical controversy. Their purpose is not to prove but rather to clarify. Just as the exercise of imagination in the earlier case of "robot rights" served a rational purpose, so it does in other areas of philosophy, too!

What Does Adopting a "Philosophical Attitude" Mean? While part of the answer to this question has already been given, it merits its own consideration. A philosophical attitude is quite unlike any other kind of attitude you may have adopted for other courses or areas of your life. It may also be called a "Socratic" point of view and involves several elements. It means, first of all, temporarily suspending your belief in the truth *or* falsity of certain things you may have been taught, told, or led to have some opinion about. It means questioning what may seem obvious—to you or others. It means trying to work your way through to a more adequate (or less objectionable) point of view, while realizing that in time you may need to abandon that point of view in favor of an even more adequate one. Subject to the time constraints of your course, there will always be opportunities for you to explore the pros and cons of a certain philosophical issue or argument at ever deeper levels. So adopting a philosophical attitude means that you are committing to an intellectual *process* quite far removed from the "take it or leave it" attitude you may have experienced in other contexts.

How Can You Study for Philosophy Tests?   The answer to this question is applicable to many courses. However, since philosophy presents some unusual challenges for the beginning student, a brief review may be useful.

1. Keep up with your assignments on a daily basis and immediately ask questions when you don't understand something. Philosophical arguments and counterarguments build logically upon one another. You might be able to memorize many facts the night before the test. However, it is far less likely that you will understand what you've committed to memory if you have not kept up. Philosophy is more like mathematics than history in this regard.
2. Review your text and class notes to make certain that you can define and understand every new term or phrase you've encountered. If necessary, make a separate list. (The Glossary at the end of this text may supplement your efforts.)
3. When a major philosophical position or claim is put forth, make sure that you can state the relevant arguments in support of the claim and the criticisms of that claim or of its supporting arguments offered by the philosophers you have been studying. Writing these on a separate sheet of paper is often helpful.
4. Comparing and contrasting the philosophical positions on a certain issue you've been studying are always useful exercises. For example, how do stoics and hedonists define the "good life"? Again, preparing brief lists will help focus your attention on the core elements of each position.
5. One very useful exercise is to place the key ideas you've been studying in separate boxes and then to draw arrows between the boxes indicating what type of relationship exists between the ideas. For example, is the idea in one box logically incompatible with one in another box? Does it logically imply or entail the truth of an idea in a third box? Or is it simply contingently related to a fourth idea?

6. Finally, the ultimate self-test in preparing for an examination is whether you can clearly and succinctly explain all of the above in your own words to another student in that class. Talking out ideas in small study groups, assuming everyone comes prepared, is both an effective and an easy way to prepare for a test.

Study Questions

We have covered a good deal of territory in this first chapter. The following study questions should help you focus upon the main topics of discussion. If you have difficulty in answering any of these questions, you may consult the appropriate discussion in the text.

1. What does it mean to say that your philosophy essay exams as a rule will be graded objectively?
2. What characteristics of philosophical problems are cited in this chapter?
3. What is a "fundamental idea"?
4. What does it mean to say that philosophical problems involve logical relations between ideas?
5. Give some examples of kinds of logical relations.
6. Give an example of an incompatibility of beliefs that contributes to a philosophical issue.
7. Distinguish between a question of principle and a question of fact.
8. What does it mean to say that philosophical problems are nonempirical?
9. What does it mean to say that a belief is empirically falsifiable?
10. Why is it false to assert that science is about an observable world and philosophy is about an unobservable world?
11. Roughly describe the relation between empirical facts and philosophical arguments. Give an example.
12. What is the difference between giving reasons and giving causes for a belief?

Postscript: Divisions of Philosophy

One time-honored approach to explaining philosophical subject matter is to present brief definitions of its divisions together with specific examples of philosophical problems. While it leaves something to be desired, this approach does give a general idea of the breadth and complexity of philosophical subject matter. Following are some historically important divisions of philosophy. (Important specialty areas, such as philosophy of mathematics, philosophy of history, philosophy of education, and biomedical ethics, are not included.)

1. *Logic* A study of the principles by which we distinguish sound from unsound reasoning and of different types of reasoning. For example, what is the difference between deductive and inductive thinking? Why is the argument "All dogs are cats; Socrates is a dog; therefore, Socrates is a cat" valid? How does the logic of scientific explanation differ from the logic of moral judgments? (Note: Some branches of logic are closer to mathematics than to philosophy. Yet it is philosophers who traditionally have taught and investigated logic and who have advanced it to its present state.)

2. *Ethics* A study of the concepts and principles that underlie our evaluations of human behavior. How ought we to behave? Is pleasure the only basis for describing a state of affairs as "good"? Is moral decision arbitrary?

3. *Metaphysics* A study of the most fundamental questions about the nature of reality that science cannot resolve. Can people exercise freedom of choice? Does God exist? Is reality essentially spiritual or material? Is the mind distinct from the body?

4. *Epistemology* A study of the origin, nature, and extent of knowledge. Is experience the only source of knowledge? What makes some beliefs true and others false? Are there important questions that science cannot answer? Can we know the thoughts and feelings of other people?

5. *Aesthetics* A study of the principles that underlie our evaluations of different art forms. What is the purpose of art? What is the role of feeling in aesthetic judgment? How does one recognize a great work of art?

6. *Political Philosophy* A study of the fundamental principles of the state, particularly those involving justice, authority, liberty, and order. For example, where should the lines be drawn between the rights of the individual and the rights of government? What is the basis for any sovereign's right to govern? (Note: Although they overlap in certain respects, political philosophy should not be confused with political science; the one is essentially concerned with ideal principles, the other with the actual organization and laws of different governments.)

7. *Philosophy of Religion* A study of the nature, kinds, and objects of religious belief. What is the relation between faith and reason? What is religion? Can God be known by direct experience? Can the existence of evil be reconciled with belief in a perfect, personal God? Do religious terms have a special meaning? Are rational arguments for the existence of God sound and, if so, do they prove equally well the existence of a Goddess?

8. *Philosophy of Science*   A study of the methods, assumptions, and limits of scientific practice. Is there a single, distinctive method in science? What is the difference between a law and a theory in science? What is the nature of scientific explanation? Are science and human freedom compatible? How does science differ from pseudo-science?

9. *History of Philosophy*   A study of the emergence, examination, and evolution of philosophical ideas as found in the writings of philosophers. What similarities and differences are there in the "social contract" theories of Thomas Hobbes and John Locke? How does Aristotle's doctrine of form and matter represent a synthesis of Plato's distinction between the world of ideas and the world of appearances? In what ways have analytic philosophers changed traditional conceptions of the methods and purposes of philosophy?

II
Why Philosophize?

Now that we have an idea of the nature of philosophical problems, we should consider some of the reasons why philosophers and lay persons give critical thought to such problems. Why philosophize? This question has several interpretations, depending on your point of view. It may express a desire to know the goals philosophers pursue in their investigations. Or it may express a student's desire to know what practical gain philosophy offers. Or from the point of view of someone already deeply involved in philosophy, the question itself may be unimportant. Accordingly, we shall survey three different responses to the question "Why philosophize?"

How Philosophers See Their Goals

The major concern of philosophers is to understand philosophical issues and to discover their most rationally defensible answers irrespective of any practical benefits. Philosophers generally agree that the pursuit and attainment of knowledge are themselves important goals. Attempting to answer a question such as "In what sense do numbers exist?" is obviously not an activity designed to acquire more friends, influence more people, eradicate poverty, or develop a technology for controlling pollution; it simply expresses the desire to investigate a philosophical problem for its own sake.

Nevertheless, doing philosophy can and does have broad, long-range "practical" benefits. Where philosophers disagree is over the precise consequences philosophical knowledge ought to have for such areas as personal happiness and action, society, and education. To appreciate some of these consequences, we must first understand what they are not; we must first clear up some misconceptions of the purpose of philosophy.

Misconceptions of Philosophy's Purposes   First, it is not the purpose of philosophy to compete with science. Two disciplines compete only when their subject matter is in principle the same. The conceptual issues that concern philosophers, however, differ in kind from the natural processes that scientists investigate. Moreover, scientists seek to explain natural phenomena, whereas philosophers not only are in no position to do so but do not even try. Nevertheless, in a limited sense, the purposes of science and philosophy may be said to overlap insofar as each may seek knowledge for its own sake. Let us see how.

Scientific explanation embodies two specific purposes, one practical, the other theoretical. The practical purpose is to predict and control. By discovering how to predict the occurrences of earthquakes, for example, scientists will be able not only to save lives and property but eventually, perhaps, to control some of the causes of earthquakes.

The other purpose of science is to achieve theoretical understanding for its own sake. For chemists, for example, it is not enough to know that two chemicals will react in a certain way under given conditions; they want to discover the ultimate structure of matter so that they can understand why that reaction takes place. Scientists are motivated not only by practical considerations, such as the need to develop a cure for cancer, but also by sheer curiosity and the satisfaction of knowing what the universe is like. Discovering the age of the universe may or may not have practical value someday. But even without assurances that it would, the astrophysicist would probably continue to investigate simply because of a desire to know. Therefore, it is a mistake to distinguish between philosophy and science on the grounds that the former has essentially impractical purposes whereas the latter has altogether practical purposes. Their purposes may often be similar, even though the kind of knowledge each seeks is different.

Second, it is not the purpose of philosophy to compete with theology. Theologians, like philosophers, do support various views with rational thought, and they do examine nonempirical issues that fall outside the scope of science. Moreover, theology has changed fundamentally in the past several decades, drastically reshaping many traditional views of its scope and purpose. Nevertheless, philosophy and theology, though comparable, have different goals.

Traditional theology is *revealed* or *natural*. In revealed theology reason functions to interpret and defend dogmas whose truth is taken on faith. Here the purposes of theology and philosophy are fundamentally opposed. Philosophers do not accept inherited beliefs as a matter of faith.

In natural theology certain central beliefs, particularly those pertaining to the existence of God, are supported with rational arguments, independent of faith and authority. At this point the subject matter and methods of natural theology partly overlap with those of philosophy, since philosophers are interested in rationally evaluating, supporting, or criticizing any argument for the existence of God. But philosophers and theologians engage in these activities for fundamentally different purposes.

In philosophy knowledge is often sought for its own sake. In natural or revealed theology it is sought principally as a means to achieve what religion takes to be humanity's final happiness or destiny; if people can be shown by reason that God exists, then they will perhaps be that much closer to accepting particular scriptures and attaining spiritual contentment. Theologians work within a framework that they are already largely committed to. This framework directly or indirectly shapes their thinking.

The central articles of religious tradition may of course be questioned. A modern Christian theologian might even question the divinity of Christ.[1] The theologian will nevertheless believe that there is something supremely compelling about his life and teachings. Philosophers, however, ideally begin their investigations from a position of intellectual neutrality, regardless of their personal sympathies or prior commitment to a religious tradition. They are, of course, influenced by the frameworks within which they work, but in the case of conflict, reason has the final say; every known assumption must be examined.

Finally, even though philosophers are sometimes rightly called on as experts on ethical decisions, it is not the purpose of philosophy actively to promote individual or social change. Contrary to the persisting misconception, philosophers do not have the "inside story" on what life is all about. Nor as a rule do they pretend to. Almost every teacher of philosophy at some time has been struck dumb by such requests as "You're a philosopher; tell me what I should do" (divorce my husband, divorce my wife, break the picket line, join the revolution, get my fifteen-year-old daughter a prescription for birth-control pills). The purpose of philosophy should not be confused with that of the minister, the politician, the psychoanalyst, or the personal advisor. Illuminating an

---

[1]This is particularly true of some recent theologians who are less concerned with questions of existence or truth, such as "Is it true that Christ is the son of God?" than with the relevance or "existential" significance of the Gospels for contemporary life. For example, the emphasis may be placed on applying Christian principles to personal and social problems rather than on believing in God. See Paul Tillich, *The Dynamics of Faith* (New York: Harper & Row, 1957), and Harvey Cox, *The Secular City* (New York: Macmillan, 1966).

ethical decision is one thing; promoting it in certain social or political circles is quite another.

Philosophers often focus critical attention on the principles that underlie alternative actions. For example, they may argue for the adoption of certain views that may lead to personal reorientation (such as leaving the church) or to political change (such as reordering national priorities). But these are different matters from personally urging Jones to lobby for the passage of the Equal Rights Amendment. Philosophers are occasionally in a position to recommend a particular course of action—for example, to advise a student about some moral dilemma. But if they choose this more active role, they do so as individuals and not because counseling is part of the philosopher's job. In summary, philosophers are necessarily thinkers and only in a secondary, or contingent, sense doers. A philosopher who ceases to think ceases to be a philosopher, but one who does not actively attempt to make the world better does not cease to be a philosopher.

When it comes to identifying the positive purposes of philosophy, philosophers begin to disagree. We are mainly concerned in this text to dispel certain misconceptions of philosophy and its purposes. But you will no doubt realize as you investigate particular issues that different philosophers themselves have a variety of outlooks. A brief survey of three important outlooks—the traditional, the analytic, and the existential—will fill out our preliminary sketch of the scope of philosophy. Historically, these views overlap. They are not necessarily incompatible, and many philosophers do not fit neatly into one tradition alone. Furthermore, no one view should be thought superior to the others. In philosophy, we cherish different ways of thinking.

The Traditional View   What we shall call the traditional view is actually a loosely knit group of assumptions spanning the history of Western philosophy—with some important offshoots along the way.[2] It has three dominant characteristics. The first is an emphasis upon broad conceptual frameworks and general principles, which served to discard false beliefs and to unify fragmented beliefs in art, science, religion, and society. The root question in this tradition is, "How does it all fit together?" For example, it was not enough for Plato (427–347 B.C.) merely to develop an adequate definition of

---

[2]For a very useful and detailed survey of the scope and influence of the traditional view, consult John Passmore's article "Philosophy," in the *Encyclopedia of Philosophy*, ed. Paul Edwards (New York: Macmillan, 1967). For a clear but narrowly conceived defense by a contemporary philosopher working within that tradition, see Blanchard's "In Defence of Metaphysics," in *Metaphysics: Readings and Reappraisals*, ed. W. E. Kennick and M. Lazerowitz (Englewood Cliffs, N. J.: Prentice-Hall, 1966), p. 331.

justice. In the process, he found it necessary to relate the results of his analysis to many other topics (including knowledge, power, moral goodness, functional harmony, and the educated person); a synthesis of the topics appears in the *Republic*, his classic view of a utopian society. The vocabulary of traditional philosophy includes many philosophical isms—for example, **'materialism'**, **'idealism'**— some of which you may have learned about in other courses. Because it tends to translate isolated beliefs and concepts into a unified world view, such philosophy is sometimes described as "speculative philosophy" or "philosophy in the grand style."

A second distinctive feature of the traditional view is its fundamental assumption that there are objective philosophical truths distinct from those of common sense and science. The purpose of philosophy should be to discover these truths. Of course, philosophers in this tradition have advanced very different theories of reality, knowledge, and morality, but these differences are assumed to be eventually reconcilable.

A third distinctive feature is an emphasis on rationally determining moral and social principles, which in turn justify our choices to behave in certain ways. This is exemplified in the famous precept of Socrates (470–399 B.C.) that "the unexamined life is not worth living." Specific moral and political action—for example, acts of civil disobedience— should be guided by reason, not whim or desire for personal gain. Thus, for those philosophers who hold the traditional view, there is a close connection between knowledge and action. Philosophers as diverse as Aristotle, Karl Marx (1818–1883), and John Dewey (1859–1952) all believed that the knowledge achieved in philosophical investigation should be beneficial to individuals and to society. Knowledge and action are, and ought to be, closely related.

Although it is not an essential part of the traditional view of philosophy, Socrates' conception of the educational process merits attention because it was an early and decisive contribution to Western philosophy in general. Socrates (whose teachings and life influenced Plato) argued that we are born with an innate knowledge of many fundamental ideas from every area of study. The educational process should therefore not be seen as a transmission of knowledge from the teacher to the student—except, perhaps, in the sense of filling in the details. Rather, the instructor should help students discover the truth within themselves and should bring their innate understanding to the surface by skillful use of a question-and-answer technique; this is known as Socratic dialogue or dialectic. Socrates is often accused of having furnished more questions than answers. But he saw himself as an "intellectual midwife" and a gadfly whose purpose was to sting people to think for themselves by asking the right questions. All philosophers, no matter what their orientation, agree with this, and part of the Socratic attitude will no doubt carry over in your class.

The Analytic View The analytic conception of philosophy poses objectives that in some ways contrast sharply with those of the traditional view.[3] Its emphasis is not on fitting the pieces (isolated beliefs and concepts) into a picture of the whole (employing unifying principles) but rather on clarifying the pieces in the first place. Along with this emphasis is the conviction that many of the problems and theories of traditional philosophy result from linguistic confusions because words and sentences that appear to imply one thing may actually imply something quite different. The purpose of philosophy should be to tackle the problem by exposing these confusions and analyzing the key concepts.

Consider the following example. The two sentences "John is tall" and "John is good" have the same grammatical form. Both ascribe adjectives 'tall' and 'good' to their subject ('John'). It is therefore easy to assume that both terms denote properties, tallness and goodness, of John—something that John may have or not have. But what type of property is goodness? Unlike tallness, it is certainly not measurable. Perhaps 'good' denotes a nonempirical property beyond the scope of science. But how do we know that John does or does not have this property? By a special faculty of moral intuition? Suppose your intuition conflicts with mine. We seem to be in a jam. One way out of the jam is to inquire whether 'is good' ascribes a property at all, despite its grammatical similarity to 'is tall'. Perhaps the meaning of 'is good' is not so much descriptive—which sends us in search of an alleged property it names—as commendatory; that is, to say "John is good" would be to say "I recommend John to you." The central contribution of analytic philosophy to the history of philosophy has been to increase our awareness of the meanings of words as they pertain to many philosophical problems.

During the heyday of analytic philosophy several decades ago, its practitioners held that philosophers should first and foremost clarify meaning rather than seek new truths about reality; philosophy should not so much add to our knowledge of the world as help us reevaluate what we already claim to know or what we assume uncritically.

---

[3]Analytic philosophy is a twentieth-century movement; it began with the writings of G. E. Moore and Bertrand Russell and includes such later philosophers as A. J. Ayer, Ludwig Wittgenstein, Gilbert Ryle, and John Austin. In one form or other, analytic philosophy is the dominant current trend in Anglo-American philosophy. Helpful surveys are found in Morris Weitz's article "Analysis," in the *Encyclopedia of Philosophy*, ed. Paul Edwards (New York: Macmillan, 1967), and in his collection of readings, *Twentieth-Century Philosophy: The Analytic Tradition* (New York: Macmillan, 1966). Several good overviews of analytic philosophy are found in G. J. Warnock, *English Philosophy Since 1900* (New York: Oxford University Press, 1958); in selected chapters of John Passmore, *One Hundred Years of Philosophy*, 2nd ed. (New York: Basic Books, 1966); and in D. J. O'Connor, ed., *A Critical History of Western Philosophy* (New York: Free Press, 1964).

Rejecting the traditional view, they also held that philosophers should not formulate standards of value, suggest how people ought to behave, argue for the best political system, or tell us what makes some art great. Philosophers, they urged, have no special competence in interpreting values—beyond analyzing their logical characteristics.

In recent years this attitude has substantially changed. Analytic philosophy retains its technically rigorous methods, but it has returned to a more traditional conception of philosophy's purpose. To be sure, the emphasis upon meaning is still there, but it is balanced by a renewed search after moral, political, and metaphysical truth. Philosophers, it is agreed, do have special critical abilities for dealing with moral and social issues. Although this shifting orientation may suggest a contradiction, it simply reflects the need for a balanced perspective. Any theoretical discipline evolves, and philosophy is no exception.

Existentialism   Existentially oriented philosophers are not particularly concerned with logically maneuvering various concepts and principles into a coherent world view or with analyzing definitions of words.[4] Rather, they want to describe what may be broadly conceived as the "human condition." In this respect, much traditional and analytic philosophy is of little relevance for the important questions of human existence. For example, a prime question for the existentialist is neither "How can I rationally prove or disprove the existence of God?" nor "What does the term 'God' mean?" Rather, it is "Does it matter whether God exists?" or "Of what relevance to my life is God, one way or the other?" Thus, existential philosophy embraces questions of psychology and personal involvement.

The existentialist view of philosophy's purpose derives from the assumption that most of us, philosophers included, have lost our sense of what it means to be a human being. We have thrown away our freedom, invented institutions and ideologies to conform to, become passive

---

[4]The existential tradition begins in the nineteenth century with Soren Kierkegaard and Friedrich Nietzsche; it includes in the twentieth century Martin Heidegger, Jean-Paul Sartre, Gabriel Marcel, and Karl Jaspers. In the twentieth century, existentialism was closely related to a distinctive view of philosophical method called **phenomenology** (the science of pure description). In different forms, these schools represent the dominant trend in Europe. A good collection of representative readings is given by Robert C. Solomon, ed., *Existentialism* (New York: Modern Library, 1974). A short survey of existentialist themes is found in Alasdair MacIntyre's article "Existentialism," in the *Encyclopedia of Philosophy*, ed. Paul Edwards (New York: Macmillan, 1967). For a longer discussion, consult Robert B. Olsen, *An Introduction to Existentialism* (New York: Dover, 1962). Less accessible, a delightful overview that makes particular reference to contemporary literature is Gordon Bigelow's "A Primer of Existentialism," in *College English* (December 1961).

automatons, and overlooked the deeper, more personal elements of existence. "To be," for contemporary people, is "to possess and to belong." Accordingly, the purpose of philosophy ought to be to wake us up, to sharpen and readjust our perception of existence. Not surprisingly, the topics of love, death, personal identity, the necessity of choice, alienation, personal communication, and alternative lifestyles occupy primary positions in existential literature over those of knowledge, logic, causality, and goodness. The purpose of existentialist philosophy is not to solve intellectual riddles or to achieve understanding merely for its own sake but to sensitize us to the conditions that affect our actions and our lifestyles. In this limited respect, existentialism is a radical wing of the traditional view; that is, the measure of philosophy's worth is the difference it makes in one's life.

Given the concerns described here, we might well expect the existentialists to offer specific answers to the question "What is the right thing to do?" Unfortunately, none is forthcoming, at least not in the form of rationally supported moral and social standards. Contrary to the traditional view, which offers numerous principles for rationally justifying specific actions, existentialists do not believe that such justification is possible, or in some cases even desirable. In the end, reason cannot ensure that this or that moral act is better than its alternatives. We must simply make the best choice we can.

The Relevance of Philosophy

For many people the question "Why philosophize?" expresses a practical interest, namely, "What's in philosophy for me, besides the pursuit of knowledge for its own sake?" There is a practical response to this interpretation. A critical involvement with philosophy can change our fundamental beliefs, including both our general view of the world and our system of values. And a change in either of these can change our personal happiness, our goal within a chosen profession, or simply our general lifestyle. But such benefits are generally the by-products, not the specific goals, of philosophical investigation.

The Practical Relevance of Philosophical Commitment   We can easily cite examples of the practical relevance of taking a philosophical stand. If, for instance, there are no truly free actions, then we should rethink our positions on criminal rehabilitation and capital punishment. (Why punish people who can't help anything they do?) To use another example, our voting preferences for issues and candidates may be deeply affected by our commitment to certain political philosophies. Again, if beauty is indeed in the eye of the beholder, how can we justify awarding prizes for the "best" work of art? And certainly our conception of immoral behavior can have far-reaching consequences for our personal relationships.

As a further example, if we were to see ourselves as an integral part of nature, then perhaps we should be less inclined to conquer it—and less likely to suffer the resulting environmental destruction. And if our Western world view were "easternized" somewhat, perhaps we should have less difficulty in explaining or accepting the phenomenon of acupuncture. These are only a few of the ways in which studying philosophical issues may be relevant to everyday life. But if you still doubt the applicability of philosophy to real-life problems, you may wish to consult some of the articles in the journal *Philosophy and Public Affairs*. Here are some examples:

- "IQ: Heritability and Inequality, Part 1" (vol. 3, no. 4)
- "War and Innocence" (vol. 5, no. 1)
- "Euthanasia" (vol. 6, no. 2)
- "Paternalistic Behavior" (vol. 6, no. 1)
- "Self-Respect and Protest" (vol. 6, no. 1)
- "Excusing Rape" (vol. 5, no. 4)
- "Justifying Reverse Discrimination in Employment" (vol. 4, no. 2)
- "Missiles and Morals: A Utilitarian Look at Nuclear Deterrence" (vol. 11, no. 3)

Before we continue, a word of caution is necessary. The causes of a change in one's fundamental beliefs are often a matter not for philosophical but for psychological investigation and cannot be controlled by philosophers. Such changes may indeed result from philosophy, just as they may result from studying other subjects or from such conditioning influences as peer-group pressure. But a critical involvement with philosophical problems does not guarantee that beliefs will change. Nor is there a way to ensure that any changes that occur are desirable. Some people find, for example, that their religious beliefs are strengthened by studying philosophy, others that their convictions are shaken. Philosophers do not try to produce either reaction.

The Practical Relevance of Philosophical Examination You are likely to benefit not only from philosophical involvement in general but also from philosophical examination in particular. Effective philosophical examination is broad, it is deep, and it is critical. The practical relevance of such examination is unmistakable. Briefly, it can increase your intellectual independence, tolerance for different points of view, and freedom from dogmatism.

First, such traits may be developed by the *breadth* of your philosophical studies. Consider the question "What makes right actions right?" Many responses may at first seem plausible: the amount of happiness generated by a particular action, self-interest, survival of the species, the dictates of one's conscience, or what society says is right. None of these alternatives is a sacred cow to which all philosophers are committed. Probably no other discipline is so devoted to impartial, rigorous examination of "the other guy's point of view." That point of view may seem unlikely, but it often can be supported with very good arguments. Discovering that there are other well-supported views besides your own can be both a frustrating and a liberating experience; either way, this discovery promotes tolerance and freedom from dogmatism.

Second, you will gain intellectual freedom and related traits by pursuing philosophical issues *in depth*. In a philosophy course you have the opportunity to investigate themes that too often get a superficial presentation in other courses. Introductory science courses, for instance, frequently point out that science is based on the principle of determinism, the belief that every event is caused. In sociology or anthropology courses the thesis that morals vary in different cultures is sometimes cited as evidence for the controversial claim that right and wrong are simply matters of individual or social preference. In an art course a fellow student may propose that there are no criteria for distinguishing good from bad art; one either likes what one sees or one doesn't. Each of these claims—and we could present many others—is pregnant with assumptions, implications, and ambiguities that are usually unaddressed; such claims are often uncritically regarded as "the truth." Philosophy invites you to examine, to call the bluff on, accepted dogmas; it invites you to take a stand.

This brings us to a third essential of philosophical examination, *critical evaluation*. The purpose of a philosophy course is not merely to survey different theories; it is also to evaluate them. Whatever your final judgment about a particular issue may be, you can develop a generally critical attitude. This means taking less for granted on the basis of authority alone, noting assumptions and ambiguities in questionable claims (including your own), refusing to be carried along by the general drift of opinion, and requesting clarifications and reasons for what may seem obvious to others. These are the ingredients of intellectual independence. *The heart of philosophy consists in shaping one's mind, not in filling it with facts.*

In summary, serious study of philosophical problems can be personally relevant in two ways. First, it may lead to a change in fundamental beliefs and values, which in turn may influence the direction of one's personal or professional life. Second, it can engender freedom from dogmatism, tolerance for opposing points of view, and intellectual independence. As pointed out earlier, there is no guarantee that philosophical investigation will have any of these effects. There are certainly other influences that contribute to tolerance and intellectual independence or that can change one's values and fundamental beliefs. Philosophy simply happens to be one of the best.

All well and good, you may say, but what about "real" practical benefits of studying philosophy—like getting a job! Well, a bachelor's degree with a major in philosophy will not train you for any specific job beyond preparing you for graduate training and teaching. But this is true of most liberal arts majors. Philosophy has the edge in equipping you for a variety of nonacademic disciplines and in many cases can help you advance within your chosen career.

Positions of responsibility and leadership in most careers—medicine, law, theology, business, and the like—require that you grapple with philosophical problems. Philosophy majors tend to do well in these careers, especially on some of the tests (GRE, LSAT, etc.) required for entrance to professional schools. Anyone can memorize facts—which is what you do in most of your undergraduate courses anyway. But jobs in the real world require much more if you are to excel. The "facts" need to be questioned, reorganized, viewed in different perspectives, thrown out the window, brought back in, tested, and thought through—logically, clearly, and innovatively. And the ability to do all this is what training in philosophy helps to develop, no matter where the facts come from.

The Lure of Philosophical Issues

A third response to the question "Why philosophize?" is, "Because you may find yourself already unconsciously involved with a philosophical problem; some philosophical problems you can't help investigating." Even though you may not have any general interest in studying philosophy, there are some philosophical issues that will inevitably interest you. What these problems are will of course vary from one person to the next. You may find yourself lured into a philosophical discussion even though the issue perhaps does not seem to be "philosophical" at all. Philosophy student or not, you may be led to do some philosophical thinking. In short, everyone carries some philosophical assumptions or beliefs. The question is not whether to deal with them, but how.

The lure of philosophy often entails becoming sensitized to matters we just had not thought about before. Many of us grew up repeating the Lord's Prayer in school each morning without thinking how atheists, Jews, or other non-Christians felt about it. Some parents still lecture their children on the evils of smoking marijuana—and then prepare for the second cocktail party of the week. We live in a supposedly free-enterprise system—where big and powerful corporations can receive special consideration from the government while smaller companies decay. Equal justice under the law? Sure, we are all for it, even though the rich stand a better chance of avoiding prosecution than do the poor. UFO advocates? Crazy bunch, aren't they? But their chances of massive culture shock are much less than ours, if and when it is discovered that "we are not alone" in the universe. Down here at the grassroots level are the makings of big philosophical issues.

The desire to become philosophically involved is often stimulated when one is confronted with an assertion that seems flatly mistaken. For instance, many of us would be deeply troubled by an unsupported statement that "No one should be held responsible for his or her actions." To take a different example, what atheist wouldn't become aroused by a claim such as "God exists, and I've got the arguments to prove it"? If the claim in question is supported with what appear to be plausible arguments, the situation can be especially frustrating. One may find oneself thinking that a certain claim can't be true, yet recognize that there seem to be good reasons for believing that it is.

Even those who have no inherent interest in general philosophical theories can become interested in one or more philosophical problems. In principle, then, a primary purpose of an introductory philosophy course is to survey representative philosophical problems. The theories, often complex and strangely worded, are unlikely to stimulate interest until one has seen how these theories are responses to legitimate philosophical problems in which one has already become interested. After all, there is little point in presenting answers to questions that have not yet been asked.

Philosophers, like other professionals, often write in a specialized language to defend and evaluate competing theories. And the theories in question will often represent reactions to still other issues. But no matter how complex or involved philosophical theories become, they are responses to problems ultimately linked to the familiar contexts of art, morality, science, religion, and common sense. At the edges of these familiar areas philosophers discover latent problems; they do not invent them out of nothing. These familiar areas harbor the problems most likely to draw one into a general study of philosophy.

To illustrate some of the preceding points, let us see how non-philosophers may be led into philosophical thinking, usually by an issue directly relevant to their special interests. Consider the following examples:

1. A veteran amputee who is experiencing a "phantom limb" begins to wonder if there is a part of himself outside his physical body.
2. A nuclear physicist, having determined that matter is mostly empty space containing colorless energy transformations, begins to wonder to what extent the solid, extended, colored world we perceive corresponds to what actually exists, and which world is the more "real." (One of our case studies in Chapter I)
3. A **behavioral** psychologist who is having increasing success in predicting human behavior questions whether any human actions can be called "free."

4. Supreme Court justices, when attempting to distinguish obscene and nonobscene art forms, are drawn into questions about the nature and function of art.
5. Airline passengers who, facing the prospect of increased "pat downs," begin to assert their right to privacy more.
6. An anthropologist, noting that societies have differing moral codes, begins to question whether there are any universal or absolute moral principles.
7. A politician who, faced with skyrocketing costs for treatment of the terminally ill, begins to wonder if, under certain carefully spelled out circumstances, physician-assisted suicide might be morally permissible.
8. A hospital administrator, faced with an overcrowded trauma center, is forced to choose between turning patients away and "going in the red."
9. A county commissioner, while developing new zoning ordinances, begins to wonder whether it's the effect or the intent (or both) of zoning laws that makes them discriminatory.
10. An IRS director, in determining which (religious) organizations should be exempted from tax, is forced to define what counts as a "religion" or "religious group."
11. A mother who, concerned over the spread of AIDS, begins to rethink her views on sex education.

We could continue this list of examples indefinitely. But already you can see that, given a particularly relevant problem, even the nonphilosopher is lured into a modest amount of philosophical thinking. If the nonphilosopher fails to see any purpose in the discipline, try raising a philosophical problem of special relevance to his or her interests. In examining possible responses, that person will probably discover a commitment to certain philosophical theses.

This completes our third response to the question "Why philosophize?" You may find some of the problems you encounter in your introductory course so interesting and worthy of further investigation, however, that this question will become less and less relevant. You will then find yourself on the inside of philosophy and involved with the issues, rather than on the outside, waiting to be convinced that you should participate.

Postscript: Are Gurus Philosophers?

As most of you know, gurus are spiritual masters who have allegedly achieved enlightenment and serenity. To help others attain these states, they use a variety of techniques; Zen masters, for example, use koans (riddles with no rational answers, such as "What is the sound of one hand clapping?") and meditation. Because their claims often sound profound and plausible, it is tempting to think of gurus as philosophers. Indeed, they often fit the popular image of philosophers as wise old men with beards. But there are several important differences between gurus and philosophers, and if you consider these differences, you will increase your awareness of what philosophy is all about.

Firstly, gurus offer serenity, which is a state of mind, a condition of calmness or detachment relatively unaffected by the ups and downs of life. By contrast, the purpose of philosophy is generally not to induce any particular state of mind. Of course, anything from depression to ecstasy may result from one's encounter with philosophy. In fact, a few philosophers, such as Lucretius (99–55 B.C.) and Spinoza (1632–1677), have held that peace of mind ought to be a goal of philosophical thinking. Historically, however, most philosophers have not set themselves any particular psychological goals.

Secondly, although gurus may help to enlighten us, many of their philosophical-sounding insights are closer to psychological generalizations about human nature. Consider one example. The following passage by a Zen master expresses the belief that happiness (the objective) is increased by avoiding pretense and role playing: "Without any intentional, fancy way of adjusting yourself, to express yourself as you are is the most important thing."[5]

Thirdly, gurus do make a fairly large number of philosophical claims. To assert that truth is within oneself, that selfhood is an illusion, and that reality is continually and creatively changing is to take a stand on philosophical issues. The following passage illustrates one such assertion, along with a bit of Zen irony: "Why are you unhappy? Because 99.9 percent of everything you think and of everything you do, is for yourself—and there isn't one."[6] Unfortunately, merely asserting this belief, or any others, does not make one a philosopher. To be a philosopher one must do philosophy, a standard that gurus generally fail to live up to. This is perhaps the most important difference between gurus and philosophers.

Doing philosophy involves developing and defending one's beliefs with rational argumentation. As a rule, gurus are not concerned with giving reasons for their insights. One does not debate with a guru; one requests clarification from him as an established authority, as someone who already has the truth. Indeed, many gurus are mildly amused by the conceptual problems with which philosophers struggle, and point out that genuine enlightenment is not attainable merely by thinking. Thus Don Juan in Carlos Castaneda's widely discussed works makes

[5]Shunryu Suzuki, *Zen Mind, Beginner's Mind* (New York: John Weatherhill, 1970), p. 82.

[6]Wei Wu Wei, *Ask the Awakened* (London: Routledge & Kegan Paul, 1963), p. xxi.

philosophically interesting claims but would hardly count as a philosopher. (Many would argue that he is not a guru either, at least in the traditional sense of the term. But that is another problem.)

There are, then, some important differences between gurus and philosophers. These differences in themselves do not imply anything about the merits of being either a philosopher or a guru; following or even becoming a guru can be a very worthwhile activity. Rather, a knowledge of these differences should be used merely to clarify and possibly reshape the expectations we have of both gurus and philosophers.

III
Thinking Critically:
Clearing Up Some
Misconceptions[1]

Developing skill in using the critical tools of philosophy is not an easy task. At some point you may ask yourself if it is worth the trouble. That is, will developing critical reasoning abilities enable you to solve problems and to discover the truth? Do professional philosophers actually make progress in their investigations? Can you expect to solve anything in your philosophy course? As you begin to philosophize, you may feel tempted to claim that philosophy is merely a matter of semantics or else simply a process of rationalizing those beliefs to which we are already emotionally attached. The purpose of this chapter is to respond to some of the skepticism concerning the possibility of philosophical progress and to give you a preliminary sense of what "thinking critically" means.

Philosophy Is Not Merely
Quibbling over Words

It is sometimes claimed that philosophy is little more than quibbling over the meanings of words. Sooner or later, for example, the answer to such questions as "Can a person survive the death of the body?" and "Is pornography a legitimate art form?" will depend on how we define 'person' and 'art form.' Philosophers (and students!), however, will often define

---

[1]This chapter is co-authored with Professor David Fenner of the University of North Florida.

the key terms of an issue in different ways that reflect their own views. If philosophers believe, for example, that a person can survive the death of the body, then they will define 'person' in a way that ensures that possibility. A person, they might hold, is essentially a spiritual entity distinct from its physical body. In the end, a discussion of immortality may seem to boil down to insisting that a certain definition of "person" is really the correct one. Thus, the skeptic concludes, we are not likely to make much progress in resolving this and other philosophical issues.

This argument rests on a mistaken assumption. To someone who tries to undermine a philosophical discussion by claiming, "It all depends on how you define your terms," the best response is simply, "Yes, often it does." But the discussion should not come to an end. On the contrary, it is usually just getting started. Given any two competing definitions, the question is "What reasons are there for preferring one definition to the other?" One person's definition is not always as good as another's. Further debate must determine which is more adequate. We will explore how to accomplish this in Chapter IV.

The Choice Between Competing Theories Is Based on Reason and Does Not Require Absolute Certainty

It may seem most of the solutions to philosophical problems can be supported with good arguments and, in addition, are open to significant objections. Hence, selecting this or that theory may seem arbitrary—a matter of personal preference. This conclusion rests on the mistaken assumption that philosophical truth is an all-or-nothing proposition. When it seems that complete certainty cannot be had, it's easy to assume that the view in question is no better or worse than its competitors. However, just because critics always seem to have objections, it does not follow that there are no reasons for preferring one theory over its rivals. The rational acceptability of the evidence for a philosophical thesis is primarily a matter of *degree*. There is much ground between absolute certainty and complete skepticism. You will avoid unnecessary frustration if you keep this important fact in mind. A theory that is relatively free from ambiguity, supported with sound arguments, and does not lead to highly dubious consequences is preferable to one that does not have these attributes.

Avoiding Philosophical Relativism

Beginning students of philosophy sometimes advance the following claim: "Although for Smith theory X is false, X is nevertheless true for me. Because the truth is relative to our own beliefs, each of us is correct."

Suppose theory X is that the earth is flat. If both students are correct, then the earth must be both flat and not flat (spherical). But the same thing cannot be both flat and spherical. Positions that lead to such contradictions are usually based on faulty assumptions. The culprit in this case is the failure to distinguish between *mere belief* and *true belief*. By making this distinction, we are able to avoid the consequence that two inconsistent beliefs are both true just because they are sincerely held. The evidence for the belief that the earth is spherical far outweighs the evidence available for the belief that it is not; mere belief does not support either the truth or falsity of a proposition. The qualification "for me" does not magically transform mere belief into true belief. If it did, we would not need evidence, and the distinction between reason and arbitrary whim would collapse. You must work your way through the evidence, not try to get around it just by declaring that the view in question is "true for me."

Philosophical Theories Are More Than Personal Beliefs

A related challenge to the idea of philosophical progress is the claim that the choice between competing theories is determined by an individual's conditioning and instincts. It is urged that the use of arguments in philosophy is really just a process of rationalizing the beliefs, commitments, and unconscious forces already at work in our lives. This view commonly underlies the use of ad hominem arguments, that is, attacking a person's character or personal circumstances rather than his or her arguments. It often takes the form of a tendency to predict and evaluate a person's philosophy in relation to his or her personality. We may hear it argued, for example, that since Jones is an insecure person, he is incapable of evaluating fairly any philosophical position that advocates revolution, change, and moral relativity—the very things that would make his life more insecure.

There are two responses to this line of argumentation. First, the psychology behind a person's commitment to a certain theory is irrelevant to the arguments supporting it. Citing various psychological factors that may motivate one toward a certain philosophical commitment does not make that commitment less important or less in need of critical examination. Second, the hypothesis of "psychological conditioning factors" is overly speculative (if not false) since it is impossible to specify all the factors leading to the adoption of any given view. Third, even if this hypothesis is true, it applies to everyone, not only to philosophers. Psychological and social conditioning should therefore affect the claims of art critics, mathematicians, theologians, lawyers, politicians, and physicists—not just philosophers.

Nobody questions that human beings evolved from lower forms of life on the grounds that biologists have a pathological attachment to animals. Despite their possible psychological quirks, biologists have good reasons for the theory of evolution. And here is the rub. Philosophers, too, support their positions with reasons. Whether or not these reasons are sound can be determined only by carefully analyzing the arguments themselves. Their potential defects, just like the potential merits of a scientific hypothesis, have to be shown. Rejecting them on psychological grounds would be arbitrary. The hypothesis of psychological conditioning is true, but very weak when it covers so much territory. Taken to its extreme, it suggests that all intellectual inquiry should boil down to a psychological study of the causes of different beliefs. That this does not happen means that each claim to truth, philosophical claims included, must be evaluated on its own merits and with the criteria relevant to the area in which it is made.

Finally, we should not assume that the influence of psychology on reason works only one way, for reason can influence our fundamental beliefs and attitudes. Critical examination of the arguments for and against a philosophical position can produce personal conversion and, indeed, can have many psychological consequences besides. Some attitudes may become ingrained in our character partly as a result of arguments with which we are confronted. Consider the argument "If women do the same quality work as men, they should receive equal pay, which in many cases they do not." This argument has helped to "raise consciousness" and positively change attitudes regarding the status of women in society. The distinction between the rational and emotional parts of behavior is sometimes hard to draw because reason can be influenced by and can influence many of our personal feelings and attitudes. The question of progress toward a defensible answer to a philosophical problem remains open, no matter whose personalities are involved.

Why Be Rational?

The question "Why be rational?" might express a request for a justification of the use of reason itself. As such, it would be unanswerable since it would be applicable to all the reasons given in response. No matter what reasons you gave, the skeptic could still request more reasons for the ones just offered, and so on forever. Alternatively, you cannot rationally prove that one should not be rational (in philosophy at least!) without contradicting yourself.

A more helpful response is simply to note that being rational "pays" in a broad sense of the term and that, by cutting short a philosophical debate with one-liners such as "We'll never get anywhere" or "You're just rationalizing what your parents taught you," one can cheat oneself. In the long run, it is in your interest to push the defense and criticism of a philosophical theory to its limits. It's easier, of course, to illustrate how being rational "pays" in nonphilosophical disciplines, for example, in wiping out certain diseases by applying scientific methods. It is harder to defend rationality in philosophy because the issues and arguments we encounter there are further removed from goals with which we can easily identify. But there are practical results, however far removed they sometimes seem. Our intellectual curiosity, peace of mind, moral decisions, political commitment, and scientific investigation all can be influenced by the positions we entertain on a variety of philosophical issues. The only way we can determine the nature and extent of that influence, and whether our beliefs ought to be changed, is to get on with the business of critical investigation. A "that's just your opinion" approach is either an expression of laziness or a refusal to face the consequences of rational inquiry.

None of us knows beforehand whether or not we'll be happier for calling our philosophical beliefs into question and seriously considering other alternatives. Once again, the only way to determine that is to take the risk of becoming critically involved and to embrace the mystery of philosophy eloquently expressed by Bertrand Russell: "Philosophy, if it cannot answer so many questions as we could wish, has at least the power of *asking* questions which increase the interest of the world, and show the strangeness and wonder lying just below the surface even in the commonest things of daily life."[2]

Critical Thinking

These two words, 'critical thinking,' are used a great deal nowadays. Not only in college and university settings do we hear them; teachers in high schools, middle schools, and elementary schools are using them as well. The reason for this is that "critical thinking" may be the best tool available for dealing with both the massive amount of information now available to us and the complexity of problems that we encounter. The Internet has made information instantly available, but more basically it has offered us incredible amounts of information. Someone sifting through that information, deciding what to trust, what to believe, needs some means for sorting through it all. We need some way of determining what is worthy to be believed and what is suspect. In parallel to this, it now seems almost impossible to give quick, easy, or rote solutions for the problems we face. The level of complexity involved with so many of our current problems—ethical, social, political, and so forth—requires us to have tools for creating and developing our own solutions for working through the complex nature of problems on our own. Critical thinking deals with how we may approach

[2]Bertrand Russell, *The Problems of Philosophy* (New York: Oxford University Press, 1959), p. 16.

problems in any area of inquiry, including philosophy, and how we may call upon our own intellectual skills for solving them.

Thinking and Critical Thinking   Some people mistakenly believe that "thinking" and "critical thinking" are more or less the same thing. If one simply "thinks hard," one is thinking critically. Unfortunately, this is not the case. Thinking has to do with manipulating beliefs and with developing beliefs from experiences. Brainstorming, being creative, coming up with an idea, and choosing among preferences are all activities of thinking. But they are not activities of critical thinking. Critical thinking is "principled thinking." Critical thinking is thinking that follows a reasoned track. It is "means to ends" thinking. It is "getting from point A to point B" thinking. It is "problem-solving" thinking.

In thinking critically, one has a goal. That goal might be to answer an ethical question, it might be to decide what research material to use in a term paper, or it might be to fashion an argument to persuade a friend that a certain movie is worth watching. Since there is a goal, we want to make sure that the path we take to reach that goal is the straightest one. We want to ensure that the means we employ for reaching our desired ends are the most effective. This is what we mean by "principled thinking." In thinking critically, our thinking is purposeful. Since we are interested in achieving some goal, and we are interested in doing this effectively, we want to make certain that each step we take actually accomplishes moving us closer to our goal.

While it is possible to address the matters mentioned above without employing reason—say, by appealing to emotion—if we are interested in achieving goals in the most effective and lasting way, we will work to build sound arguments that will serve as justifications for our positions. If I can offer a good argument for my moral position on a given matter, even if others disagree with me, they can respect the fact that I have thought through the matter carefully. Moral positions not based on thoughtful consideration do not usually command such respect. If I am writing a term paper and I have made a reasoned discrimination between including materials in my research studies from academic journals and including materials taken from supermarket tabloids, my conclusions will stand on much firmer grounds. And if I can offer evidence for my claim that a certain movie is good, then my friend can see that my recommendation is not exclusively a matter of reporting my own preferences; he or she can consider the presented evidence and recognize that there are reasons for my recommending this particular movie. *Critical thinking is purposeful, goal-directed thinking that follows a principled, reasoned track.*

The Skills of Critical Thinking   There are two parts to critical thinking. The first part has to do with the *skills* of critical thinking. The second part has to do with the *spirit* to think critically.

Philosophers understand the skills of critical thinking primarily to consist in informal logic. Informal logic is presented in Chapters IV and V of this book. Informal logic relies, of course, on the methods of formal logic. The reason we call it "formal" is because logic deals with the form of arguments. It does not deal with the contents of arguments, only with their structure. Consider the following classical syllogism:

P1   All men are mortal.
P2   Socrates was a man.
C   Therefore, Socrates was mortal.

This syllogism has both a form and a content. The content deals with the morality of men and Socrates' status as both a man and a mortal being. But the form of this syllogism might be represented like this:

P1   All A are B.
P2   C is an A.
C   Therefore, C is a B.

In replacing the content terms (with variables) with letters, we emphasize the form of the argument by abstracting it from its content. We remove the content, and we are left with the form. Logic deals with this, that is, with the form of arguments. We will examine this type of structure in more detail in Chapter V.

Critical thinking skills, as expressed philosophically in informal logic, include more than simply a consideration of the structures of arguments. All arguments have forms, but all real-world, everyday arguments also have contents. Informal logic incorporates consideration of the content as well as the form. When we are talking about the contents of arguments, we are focused on whether the individual premises in an argument are worthy to be believed. In short, we are interested in whether the premises are true and, if so, *what kind of truth* they express. Again, this will be investigated in detail in Chapters IV and V. For now, the point to be made is that informal logic deals with both the form of arguments and their contents, and to the extent that we are concerned with the truth of premises, we will be focused on what evidence can be brought to bear for believing them. The more evidence, and the stronger that evidence, the more justified one will be in accepting that premise as true. Critical thinking is about both gathering and evaluating information, information which can be used as evidence for premises in arguments. Critical thinkers seek reliable sources of evidence but at the same time scrutinize for themselves what information they uncover. Reliable sources are important, but considering the evidence—the quality of the information for supporting one's claims—is a task that the critical thinker must perform for oneself individually and routinely.

When philosophers think of the skills of critical thinking as informal logic, we are essentially concerned with building quality arguments. The sort of arguments we are interested in are arguments where the premises lead a person, step by step, to the conclusion, where the truth of the premises is taken down to the conclusion so that anyone listening to this argument would see that on the strength of the premises and how they are put together, it is perfectly reasonable to believe in the argument's conclusion. We call these sorts of arguments "coherent."

"Consistency" means that two things go together without a contradiction. But "coherence" is more than this. For two things to cohere means that they not only go together without a contradiction—that they are consistent—but also support one another, that they fit together. One of the best examples of this is the crossword puzzle. Consider the following puzzle:

			M		
			A		
			D		
			R		
			I		
L	O	N	D	O	N

Even without further clues, most people will probably guess that what goes into the blanks are "P," "A," "I," and "S." What are the clues that are given? Madrid and London are European capitals, so one may expect that what letters should go into the blanks will form the name of another European capital. What are the constraints? The word must have exactly five letters, and the middle letter must be an "R." Because of both the clues and the constraints, we can work out fairly easily what letters go into the blanks. Crossword puzzles are exercises in coherence. The words support one another, and they do so by offering both clues and constraints to future candidates for correct answers.

Quality arguments are like this. Premises limit our conclusions, but they also point to them. The building of quality arguments (*sound arguments*) is what informal logic is about, and informal logic, once again, is the way that most philosophers understand the skills of critical thinking.

Nonphilosophers may rely on broader conceptions of critical thinking skills. The definition offered above—*critical thinking is purposeful, goal-directed thinking that follows a principled, reasoned track*—is meant to accommodate all conceptions. Therefore terms like "principled thinking" and "reasons" are used to signal that critical thinking need not be limited just to the philosophical skills described in logic. The application of principled scientific inquiry—what we used to refer to as scientific method—is a way to address problems in both the natural and social sciences. As this is about principled problem solving, addressing scientific problems in this way counts as critical thinking. When literary critics and art critics are offering reasons for their claims that a given work of art means one thing or another, or that a given work of art is of high artistic merit, what these critics may be described as doing is applying the skills of critical thinking. As they offer cases for their judgments, they are thinking critically. When a physician attempts to diagnose a patient's ailment, when a mathematician is constructing a proof, when a computer programmer is developing software, thinking is purposeful, goal-directed, and following a reasoned track. These are all instances of principled thinking, and as such, they are all illustrations of critical thinking.

The skills employed by scientists, critics, and computer programmers may not map precisely onto the set of skills described by philosophers in talking about informal logic, but there is bound to be a good deal of similarity. Logic describes, or codifies, the correct means of using reason. To the extent that scientists, critics, and computer programmers are using reason, and using it well, to address their respective problems, they are employing skills of logic. Add to this a concern with evidencing claims, with the truth of premises, and we have critical thinking. So while critical thinking may be applied to any and all endeavors where principled reasoning is important, the roots of critical thinking—at least of the skills of critical thinking—lie in logic.

The Spirit of Critical Thinking   Is one's possession of the skills of critical thinking sufficient to make one a critical thinker? Sadly, no. If one does not employ the skills of critical thinking, then the possession of them is only half of what is needed. To be a critical thinker means more than simply having a skill-set. It means using that skill-set each time a problem presents itself, and it means accepting the result of that work. Ultimately, to have a spirit to think critically is more than an *assent to the worthiness* of engaging in critical thinking (to use the skills of critical thinking); it is more than a *willingness* to engage in critical thinking; it is even more than an *enjoyment* of engaging in critical thinking. To have a spirit to think critically is to have the *habit* of engaging in critical thinking. Critical thinkers habitually, routinely, and frequently apply their critical thinking skills (in the weak sense) to the problems they encounter regularly in their everyday life and (in the strong sense) to their own beliefs, assumptions, and attitudes. They also accept, act on, and live by the beliefs, assumptions, and attitudes they have developed as a result of thinking critically.

Developing a well-grounded habit of thinking critically comes with constant practice, and it usually comes over time. This is why it is so important for elementary teachers to be talking about critical thinking just as much as university professors do. Perhaps the skills of critical thinking can be taught at any time, but to develop an almost instinctual reliance on critical thinking, the spirit of critical thinking needs to be fostered and nurtured as early as possible. For college students, the spirit of critical thinking may be fostered in a number of ways, some of which are mentioned at the end of this section. In general, nurturing a spirit of critical thinking requires being open and willing to both challenge and be challenged. Growth through challenge is perhaps the best way, once a person has reached college age, of enhancing a spirit of critical thinking. As one experiences more and more success with critical thinking—success measured against both reaching the problem-solving goals one faces and moving toward greater confidence with regard to the truth, consistency, and stability of one's own beliefs—one will be more apt to continue in this vein, to continue practicing being a critical thinker.

The Positive and the Negative   We often use the word "critical" to denote something negative. Certainly there is something of the negative in critical thinking, which ideally comes with a fair-minded skepticism. Critical thinkers are not quick to believe. They ask lots of questions, probe to uncover assumptions, and challenge claims and suppositions. Critical thinkers look to expose falsity. So there is something of the negative about critical thinking.

But essentially critical thinking is a positive enterprise. Critical thinkers are problem solvers. We are interested in framing approaches to meet our goals that are effective, efficient, and lasting. In turning the critical thinking spotlight on ourselves, we pursue our own growth as thinkers and, more simply still, as human beings. Critical thinkers are not easily duped. We think for ourselves; we stand behind our beliefs; we have the confidence of knowing that those beliefs of ours that have been critically tested are worthy to be believed. At the same time, critical thinkers are always open to new arguments, new evidence, and new points of view. Critical thinkers as a matter of routine not only welcome new opportunities for thinking rationally and objectively but also seek them out. Critical thinking is essentially a constructive enterprise.

"Scientific studies have shown . . . "   As noted earlier, thinking scientifically is one way to think critically. To do so involves a fairly broad range of criteria that must be satisfied in order to establish a law or a theory in the sciences. For example: Are the data both sufficient and unbiased? Are the experiments well designed? Have they been replicated? Are the investigators credible or (ideally) highly respected?

Are the results of research consistent with other well-established laws and theories? Has an adequate explanation actually been determined?

However, some people have a tendency to accept sentences beginning with "Scientific research has shown. . ." uncritically as if truth has arrived and others had best get on board. There are two precautionary notes to keep in mind here. First of all, there are plenty of studies that don't show what they claim to prove. Further research often can disprove what at first seems to be the case. Good research often takes years, if not decades. And as a group, scientists are generally no less biased, prone to error, or politically motivated than other types of thinkers. Scientists themselves have shown that approximately five to seven percent of their colleagues "fudge" their research numbers, and a few just outright lie about what they claim to have accomplished. It's useful to keep this in mind in philosophy classes, which always carry a full dose of controversial issues to examine. Controversy loves company. Consequently, the empirical evidence that is likely to play some limited role in your philosophical investigations may not be as free of controversy as the one who begins his case with "Studies have shown. . ." would like you to believe.

A second precautionary note briefly refers us back to Chapter I. Empirical evidence and scientific research in themselves cannot "solve" philosophical problems. If they could, the problems would be scientific, not philosophical, in the first place. Uncovering or citing more empirical facts will solve little in philosophical discussion, even though in some instances they are more central to the discussion than in others. For example, some philosophers interested in the nature of consciousness or "mind" have found it useful to familiarize themselves in considerable depth with research involving the brain. Together with some neurobiologists, a few have concluded that the mind is the brain and there is no "mind-body problem." Why this still is a significant problem you will likely encounter in your philosophy course. The point to remember for now is that, even if the studies cited are good by scientific standards, their relevance in philosophical discussion is limited. Scientific research and knowledge can be useful up to a point but should not be taken as the kind of critical thinking that is likely to advance a point of view significantly in philosophical investigation. Some of the types of critical thinking that are likely to do this are described in the following chapters.

Exercises

1. Consider some quick presentation of a claim that you have heard or seen: a "sound-bite," a bumper sticker, a billboard, something like that. Think through the assumptions and suppositions involved with this claim. Ask yourself if those

assumptions and suppositions can withstand challenge. For instance, consider the bumper sticker which reads "Abortion stops a beating heart." What assumptions are involved in this? If the goal of this bumper sticker is to encourage a pro-life attitude and to discourage abortion, then the key to acceptance of the goal lies in the supposition that "it is wrong to stop a beating heart." Is this the case? Is it wrong to stop a beating heart?

2. Listen to a lecture, a political speech, or a religious sermon. Try to identify the goal of the speaker. How does she move her case along, step by step, toward that goal? With what assumptions is she working? What is she asking you to accept in order for her to make her case?

3. Read a newspaper or magazine article, either in print or electronically. Such articles are not usually meant to advance particular claims, conclusions, or theses, yet they still have a goal of conveying information. Consider what evidence is being put forward to justify believing the information the article writer seeks to convey. Consider whether there are assumptions involved in accepting this information, assumptions which in the article go unmentioned or unexplored.

4. Read a philosophical argument, one perhaps from an anthology of philosophical theories. Think through how the philosopher constructs her case. Think through her suppositions, her claims, and her evidence. Think about the structure of her argument, how it progresses toward its conclusions. Finally, think of challenges that you can raise. What does accepting her conclusion commit you to? What does it imply? Does it cohere with other things you believe? Why or why not?

5. Consider what it would mean to adopt a belief not only outside of your current set of beliefs but also outside of the normal scope of your beliefs. Consider perhaps what it would mean to believe in extraterrestrial life, in ghosts, or in God—if any of these is currently outside the scope of your beliefs. What would it take for you to hold such a belief? What evidence would be required? Would you have to give up some of your present beliefs? What level of evidence and argument would be required for you to give up some of your present beliefs in order to adopt such a belief?

6. Consider what it would mean to give up one of your most central beliefs, say a belief in the physical or corporeal nature of the natural world (as we have in *The Matrix*), in biological evolution, or in God. What would it take for you to give up such a belief?

7. Finally, can you think of a (controversial) claim that seemed to have been very strongly supported by science at one time but was later falsified? Can you think of a philosophical problem in, say, religion or ethics that someone may have attempted to address mainly by appealing to scientific research and knowledge? For example, do the complex and even beautiful "laws of nature" collectively imply the existence of a supreme lawgiver?

8. Pick one of President Obama's speeches and distinguish between those parts where he attempts to *inspire* us and those where he attempts to make a case for a certain conclusion.

IV
Doing Philosophy:
Getting Started

Because philosophers do not rely on the scientific method, they must depend instead on different forms of rational investigation and evaluation. Chapters IV and V examine some basic critical tools philosophers use and offer you the means to tackle issues raised in your first philosophy course.[1] You may be surprised to learn that many of the techniques differ little from those found in other disciplines. What makes arguments "philosophical" is often the subject matter rather than some special reasoning process used only by philosophers.

Before we begin, a special word of explanation is necessary. Chapters IV and V are fairly detailed. They have more information than you can profitably absorb in one reading. Most importantly, you are not expected to understand and apply every point right away. Think

---

[1]For a useful and engaging survey of the uses and abuses of reason in nonphilosophical contexts, consult Howard Kahane, *Logic and Contemporary Rhetoric: The Use of Reason in Everyday Life*, 5th ed. (Belmont, Calif.: Wadsworth, 1988) and Robert J. Fogelin, *Understanding Arguments* (New York: Harcourt Brace Jovanovich, 1987). Many of the topics treated in these chapters are discussed in Irving Copi, *Introduction to Logic*, 6th ed. (New York: Macmillan, 1982). A readable and practical text for the beginning student who seeks a working knowledge of techniques for analyzing concepts is John Wilson's *Thinking with Concepts* (New York: Cambridge University Press, 1969). For the advanced student, more technical expositions and applications of philosophical methods are found in Samuel Gorovitz and R. G. Williams, *Philosophical Analysis: An Introduction to Its Language and Techniques*, 2nd ed. (New York: Random House, 1969), and Ian P. McGreal, *Analyzing Philosophical Arguments* (Scranton, Pa.: Chandler, 1967).

of these chapters more as long-term companions rather than as fleeting acquaintances to be summed up at a glance or quickly abandoned. Work through one section at a time. At first read for a general understanding of the key points of each section; you will find that the details will take care of themselves in time. In a few sections, further explanation by your instructor may be desirable. Working through the exercises at the end of each section will increase your understanding as well as help you translate that understanding into practical skill. Take your time, and do not expect instant success in mastering critical strategy. The purpose of this chapter is merely to help you get started doing philosophy. You will develop greater skill and understanding as you apply the critical questions to the particular issues discussed in your course. Good luck!

Preparing to Philosophize

Several preliminary matters require attention in preparing to philosophize. First, philosophizing involves four psychological traits that improve effective communication: (1) the courage to examine one's cherished beliefs critically; (2) a willingness to advance tentative hypotheses and to take the first step in reacting to a philosophical claim, no matter how foolish that reaction might seem at the time; (3) a desire to place the search for truth above the satisfaction of apparently "winning" the debate or the frustration of "losing" it; and (4) an ability to separate one's personality from the content of a discussion. The last point deserves to be emphasized; a failure to make this separation may result in cloudy thinking or a conflict of personalities that can make progress in a discussion difficult.

Second, philosophizing is a skill that must be developed with practice. It is more like the abilities of a surgeon or race-car driver than those of a computer programmer. There are few "cookbook" rules in philosophy that you can simply memorize and apply mechanically to get a quick and correct answer. Philosophical problems are diverse and slippery. Just as the race-car driver must apply a general knowledge of mechanics to shifting conditions during a particular race, you should apply our methods sensitively, with an awareness of the peculiarities and interconnections of specific issues.

Third, one does philosophy as well as studies it. This should not be confused with merely doing research and appealing to authorities, such as textbooks or arguments reported at second hand. The real "authorities," the great philosophers, must be examined to sift out the enduring truth of their views. You must do this attentively, for you cannot take much for granted as you begin to read, say, Plato or Descartes. With practice, philosophy becomes a habit of mind.

Fourth, to do philosophy, one does not just consult one's personal opinion. Personal attitudes may perhaps serve as a stimulus to your critical inquiry but never as a standard to choose between different arguments or theories. "I like this view" is never a good reason in philosophy. The important question is rather "Why do you think that this is the best position?" Exercising your own intelligence means that you do not resolve issues or build new theories merely by appealing to authority or personal opinion.

Fifth, productive philosophizing should not be confused with doing psychology. A common example of this confusion is the attempt to criticize a person's philosophical belief by attributing it to a cause in that person's past—to childhood training, social pressure, neuroses, and so forth. This is called the "genetic fallacy" (discussed more fully in Chapter V) and is particularly evident in discussions of religion and morality. If philosophers are asked, "Why does Jones believe in God?" they do not answer, "Because Jones was conditioned by his Sunday school lessons to believe in God" or "Because Jones is insecure and feels better with the idea of a father figure." In this case, philosophers are concerned not with causes but with the *reasons* that can be given for or against the belief that God exists. Again, consider the 'why' in "Why is Jones committed to such and such a political view?" It is the philosopher's job not to psychoanalyze Jones but to determine the theoretical justifications and criticisms of Jones's political view.

Sixth, philosophy has two sides, one critical, the other constructive. For example, it is one thing to criticize John Locke's social contract theory of government, and quite another to improve upon it. The methods we shall survey favor the critical side for two reasons. In the first place, we must generally learn to analyze other people's philosophical viewpoints critically before we can engage in theoretical speculation on our own account. We thereby avoid repeating others' mistakes. In the second place, criticism can itself be constructive. In exposing the weaknesses of other theories, we often find that an outline of a new and better view emerges naturally. Of course, there is no substitute for creative insight, but in philosophy such insight tends to emerge only after it has been nurtured by disciplined critical analysis.

Finally, in evaluating philosophical claims, make some attempt to gauge the relative strength of your criticisms. A very strong criticism, for example, would be that a certain theory is self-contradictory; a very weak criticism, that you must see more arguments before you are convinced. Remember, too, that philosophy is seldom an all-or-nothing proposition. A tendency for some beginning students of philosophy is to claim to have "refuted" a theory with several criticisms that often require only a modification in the theory—not its total abandonment. To put it bluntly, it is good practice to let your arguments speak for themselves. Understatement in philosophy is preferable to overstatement, for you may have to eat your words. For example, you might do well to finish your examination with something like, "It appears then, that there are three problems with theory X" (then state the problems). This is preferable to the overstatement "I conclude, then, that there is no hope for theory X" (even though in fact there may be no hope).

This much having been said to help prime you for the active use of reason, it should be emphasized that philosophy is an *intellectual passion*, not merely the abstract application of technique. To assume that logic will (or can) settle everything is to fall prey to what some philosophers have called the "illusion of technique." Philosophy is not about winning points or arguments or being clever, although you will inevitably encounter some of this. It is *caring about truth* and, as the word philosophy itself originally meant, "loving wisdom."

What Kind of Claim Is Advanced?

One of the first jobs of the philosopher is to determine exactly what type of thesis is being asserted or questioned. We need to know this in order to know how to go about examining it. After all, we would not think of evaluating a work of art in the same way that we evaluate a scientific hypothesis. The purpose of this section is to distinguish some different types of claims or questions. In what follows we shall look, in detail, at varieties of claims: the empirical, the a priori, and the normative. This section may be the trickiest of any in the chapter. However, it is not necessary that you immediately master the details and subdistinctions within each variety. That comes only with time and practice. For now, it is important that you understand the main differences between the three types of claims. So let's take them one at a time.

Is the Claim Empirical?   If a thesis can be falsified by the facts of observation or experimentation, it is empirical. This we established in Chapter I. Other terms used to describe empirical claims are '**contingent**' and '**a posteriori**', which indicate a statement whose truth or falsity is determined by experience. "Some insects are immune to nuclear radiation" is an example of such a thesis. Any debate about its truth or falsity is essentially one for simple common sense or science to resolve.

There are a number of slippery claims that often seem empirical to beginning students of philosophy but turn out not to be upon closer examination. An example is "Every event has a cause." Doesn't this assertion seem straightforwardly empirical? After all, there are causes and events in the world for all to experience; for instance, LSD sometimes causes hallucinations. Each time we discover a cause for an unexplained phenomenon, we seem to add empirical support for the thesis that all events are caused. This thesis seems unfalsifiable, however. To prove it false, you would have to come up with an event that was literally not caused. Is this possible? It appears not. If you claimed to have performed an experiment in your science lab in which an uncaused event was the result, your lab instructor would no doubt respond that you had not looked hard enough for the cause. If there must be causes for events, then the thesis "All events have causes" should not be classified as empirical, because it is not falsifiable. When we find causes, we are not actually verifying the thesis from empirical evidence; rather, we are interpreting our experience and the events in it in accordance with the principle of causality. The principle functions as a conceptual truth, part of a network of ideas that we lay over our experience to make sense of it. *It is exemplified by empirical facts, but it is not a conclusion drawn from them.*

In summary, then, the first cluster of questions that you apply to a thesis is designed to tell you whether it is empirical. Are there any observations that prove or disprove the claim? Can you test it in the laboratory and get a yes or no answer? Is there anything in experience that falsifies the claim? If the answers to these questions are all "No," the thesis in question is not empirical. And if it is not empirical, then it is either a priori or normative.

Is the Claim a Priori?   An **a priori** claim is one whose truth or falsity is not determined by experience (observation). Such a thesis is known to be true or false independently of observation or experimentation. It is known instead by reason or a kind of direct intellectual intuition. A priori claims are said to be necessary; that is, they express beliefs about what seemingly must be the case or what cannot be the case. While it is perhaps a bit oversimplified, to think of a priori claims is to think "Once true, always true, and extremely difficult, if not impossible, to conceive otherwise." Once I learned that 2 plus 2 is 4, this fact could never be falsified by experience. I may have needed to experience pictures of apples and oranges in the first grade to provide a content for learning this abstract truth of arithmetic (although it seems simple now), but once I grasped that truth it could not be overturned by something that I might have learned later. Such is the case with the previously discussed a priori truth, "Every event has a cause." To be sure, actual observable events provide a content for this claim, yet finding events to falsify it seems an impossible task. In summary, a priori claims may assume some beginnings in experience, and they may be given a content by empirical facts. But once discovered they seem to have a life of their own, independent of scientific discoveries. So much for a general description of a priori claims. Our next step is to survey different kinds of a priori claims.

1. *Definitions* Statements in which the *meaning* of a term is explicitly stated, either in whole or in part, constitute a type of a priori claim. For example, "Triangles have three sides" (part of the definition of a triangle) and "Bachelors are unmarried males" (the standard definition of a bachelor) each give us the meaning of certain terms. Definitions can be a tricky subject in philosophy, and we shall discuss them more fully later. For now, let us say that the a priori character of definitions results from our decision to count such and such as part of the meaning of a term—a decision that is reinforced by common usage in most cases.

2.   *Statements the (necessary) truth of which follows directly from the meanings of key terms*   There are some statements in which no meaning is given explicitly but whose truth can be determined merely by inspecting the implied or unstated meanings of its key terms. For example, "John cannot be an atheistic Baptist" is necessarily true, given our understanding of 'atheist' and of 'Baptist'. Because the definitions of these terms are not supplied in the sentence, we must rely on our prior understanding of their meanings. 'Baptist' means partly 'one who believes in God', while 'atheist' means 'one who believes that God does not exist'; thus we cannot apply both terms to the same person. Such a move is logically precluded by the meanings of the terms. Given those meanings, there is no way we could falsify "John cannot be an atheistic Baptist" by an appeal to observation or science. This type of a priori statement, and the definitional variety just described, is said to be *analytic,* that is, a statement whose necessary truth or falsity (as in "Triangles have four sides") derives from the meanings of key terms.

3. *Tautologies* **Tautologies** are a relatively narrow type of a priori claim, the necessary truth of which is directly tied to their logical form or to truth-functional connectives, such as 'and', 'or', and 'if–then'. There are certain unstated meanings in the background, so to speak, but unlike other a priori claims, tautologies are empty of content. Stated differently, whatever content they may embody is entirely irrelevant to the necessary truth of the form involved. Examples of tautologies are: "If $A = B$, and $B = C$, then $A = C$," and "The earth is either composed of worms or it is not" (either P or not-P).

4. *Synthetic a priori* A fourth type of a priori claim expresses a necessary truth that does not appear to depend upon the meanings of key terms or upon a particular logical form. Unlike the preceding three types, this variety typically purports to give us substantive information about the world, not merely about how we have defined certain terms. Examples of such a priori propositions are "Every event has a cause," "Moral responsibility presupposes freedom of action," and "Colors have dimension." To be sure, the necessary truth of these propositions assumes that we understand the meanings of the key terms. But these meanings are not tied to each other as were, for example, 'bachelor' and 'unmarried male'. Consider the third proposition, "Colors have dimension." We can understand what dimension is without an attending definition of color, and vice versa. The key terms in this case are defined independently of each other.[2]

---

[2]Some philosophers describe this fourth type of a priori claim as "synthetic" and the first three types as "analytic." The denials of analytic a priori statements are self-contradictory and those of synthetic a priori statements not self-contradictory. The question of whether all a priori statements are analytic or whether some may be synthetic is controversial. In general, this distinction is best left to further discussion by your instructor.

Is the Claim Normative? Both empirical and a priori claims have a common function: to state facts and give information. What they give us information about—for example, the natural world or the way words are defined—may be open to debate. But their intent is to tell us what is the case. In this they differ strongly from normative claims, or claims you would usually call "value judgments." Normative claims are found in almost every academic discipline, although they are studied most intensely in the philosophical areas of ethics, aesthetics, and political theory. While they may have an information-stating function, their distinctive function is prescriptive.[3] They are essentially guides for attitudes and behavior. Typically, the person who makes a normative claim is recommending that a certain attitude or course of action be taken. Whether we take the advice depends in part upon the reasons given for the recommendation.

Simple examples of normative claims are "Osama bin Laden was an *evil* person," "Everyone *ought* to look out for himself," "Everything in the contemporary art section is *great*," and "When in doubt, the *right* thing to do is to consult your conscience." As these examples suggest, normative claims may be expressed in the form of general principles or particular judgments. For instance, "One ought never to lie, except to save another's life" applies to everyone in general and to no one in particular. On the other hand, "Jones did the wrong thing in lying" expresses a particular moral judgment about Jones. In either case, the primary intent is to guide, prescribe, and commend; that is, both are normative claims.

It is tempting to think of normative claims as a special kind of a priori claim. After all, a moral judgment is not empirically falsifiable, which is one of the marks of the a priori claim. (To be sure, empirical facts are absolutely vital in examining moral claims, but they do not play the decisive role here that they do in science.) There is a critical difference, however. A priori claims (as well as empirical claims) are primarily information-giving or fact-stating. They purport to tell us the way things *are*. On the other hand, even though they may indirectly convey some information, normative claims purport primarily to tell us the way things *ought* to be. Neither a priori nor empirical claims exhibit this prescriptive function.

Normative claims are not always full-blown and easily recognizable. Sometimes we have to coax them to the surface from the context in which they are buried. For example, some statements may have an empirical interpretation in one context and a normative interpretation in another. Consider "Everyone does it." This might be viewed as a

---

[3]The status of normative claims is controversial. However, there appears to be general agreement that their function is not merely or straightforwardly fact stating as, for example, empirical claims are.

simple statement of fact. Perhaps everyone is doing it, whatever "it" may be—politicians accepting favors, for example. In a different context, the claim might function as a *normative justification* for someone's getting in on the action; "If everyone else is doing it, then it's OK for me to do it also." Here the speaker is not merely describing but prescribing acceptable courses of action. Similarly, the statement "Terrorism must be wiped out," considered by itself, essentially expresses a moral judgment about something that *ought* to be done. Yet, it could be connected to other concerns that make it more empirical—for example, "If we are to fly (open our mail, etc.) safely, then terrorism must be wiped out." This latter statement may be debatable, but is primarily fact-stating, not normative, in its intent.

The Claims: A Summary

By now you are probably saturated with new terms and distinctions. To help clarify matters, some main points are summarized in the following outline:

I. *Empirical.* Empirical knowledge involves a posteriori beliefs about what contingently happens to be the case; the beliefs are based upon experience.
    A. One type is determined by simple observation or by generalizing from observed data. Examples: "My arm is bleeding," "All crows are black."
    B. A second type is determined by experimenting with hypotheses. Example: "Low blood sugar causes depression."

II. *A Priori.* A priori knowledge involves beliefs about what necessarily is or is not the case. They are not based upon experience and are not falsifiable by experience.
    A. One type is *tautologies*. Their truth or falsity is determined purely by examining their logical form. Example: "If $A = B$, and $B = C$, then $A = C$."
    B. A second type is *definitions*. Here the meaning of a term is expressly stated. Truth or falsity is determined by methods we shall describe in the following section. Example: "A bachelor is an unmarried male" (analytically true).
    C. A third type includes claims whose truth or falsity is determined by the *unstated meanings* of the key terms. Example: "John cannot be an atheistic Baptist" (analytically true).
    D. A fourth more controversial type involves statements whose truth or falsity appears not to depend on the meanings of the key terms. Example: "Every event is caused."

III. *Normative.* In contrast to empirical and a priori claims, normative claims prescribe what ought to be the case, not merely what is believed to be the case. They may be expressed as general principles or particular judgments, or they may be part of an unstated interpretation buried in, say, an empirical context. Because they are prescriptive or behavior-guiding does not mean that they are arbitrary or purely subjective. Normative claims can be, and frequently are, defended with reasons. Examples: "One ought never to kill another human being, except in self-defense." "Everyone knows science is (ought to be?) free of value judgments."

This preceding summary still covers a lot of territory. With practice and exposure, you will feel more comfortable with the details. At this point, you should concentrate on the three basic types of claims. You should be able to state in a sentence or so (1) what an empirical claim is, (2) what an a priori claim is, and (3) what a normative claim is. For practice, let us see how the types we have surveyed may be applied to some specific cases, remembering that without a complete context some of our analyses will be open to interpretation. Each of the following claims involves the concept of morality, but in quite different and overlapping ways:

1. All children in Nigeria receive moral training.
2. There are no selfless moral actions.
3. A moral person is one who examines his or her conscience.
4. Promise-keeping is morally right.
5. No hedonist (pleasure-seeker) can be moral.
6. No moral person does what he or she thinks is right.

The first sentence is clearly an empirical claim. It is not the philosopher's job to defend it or attack it. Any questions about its truth should be resolved by the sociologist or anthropologist.

The second sentence may look empirical, but it usually turns out not to be because it is not empirically falsifiable. Actually, the term 'moral' is largely irrelevant, since the claim is that all actions, not just moral ones, are selfishly motivated: Isn't everybody out for number one? The claim seems empirical because there are so many cases of selfish acts in the world. But this generalization is not falsifiable; exceptions to it might be ruled out on the grounds that deep down what appear to be unselfish acts are really selfish. For instance, I give my valuable time to do some charity work, but I'm really just satisfying a selfish desire to be well thought of or to ease my conscience. A few more such examples would illustrate that the second sentence is an arbitrary decree not based upon empirical investigation.

The third sentence is probably intended as a definition. As a definition, it would be very poor since some of us have corrupt consciences to examine.

The fourth sentence is a normative claim that expresses a general moral principle. Notice that if we were to assert merely that promise-keeping is *considered* moral, we would then be making an empirical claim.

With a little stretch of the imagination, the fifth sentence might be interpreted as an empirical claim about the personalities of hedonists. Perhaps they just can't bring themselves to do moral things, as 'moral' is conceived here. A more plausible interpretation would be that the statement is intended as an analytically true claim; that is, on the basis of certain presumed definitions, it asserts an incompatibility between 'hedonism' and 'morality'. For example, it is often pointed out that being moral sometimes entails rejecting pleasure in favor of duty.

The sixth sentence involves a self-contradiction. To be a 'moral person' means, in part, doing what one *believes* is right. The sixth sentence denies this and consequently is not just contingently false; it is necessarily false. (We might, of course, disagree with the person's belief, but that is another problem.)

Exercises

The exercises at the end of each section will increase your ability to apply the critical tools discussed in this chapter. Some passages of no particular philosophical interest are included intentionally to introduce you to the art from a familiar perspective. Analyzing other passages will require guidance from your instructor. A single passage may involve several defects and should be analyzed accordingly. Because the context of the claims is not given, it will be necessary for you to examine some of them in light of several possible meanings of key terms. Answers are given on page 132.

Each of the following groups involves a single key term. The claims themselves, however, are of different logical types. You are to determine whether the claim advanced is empirical, a priori (necessary), or normative. Remember that without a fuller context, some might be classified in more than one way.

A. 1. People deprived of happiness cease to care about living.
   2. You cannot find a happy person who is wholly self-centered.
   3. Happiness is the basis of all adequate moral standards.
   4. There are only two types of persons, the happy and the nonhappy.
   5. Happiness is nothing other than having one's desires fulfilled.

B. 1. What time is it?
   2. What is time?
   3. Would time pass if the universe stood still?
   4. When you are bored, does time pass slowly?
   5. Shouldn't you make better use of your time?

C. 1. Because they deal primarily with human psychology, existentialists cannot be called philosophers.
   2. Philosophy is love of wisdom.
   3. Philosophical problems cannot be solved by experiments.
   4. Philosophers are usually intelligent people.
   5. Philosophy is completely irrelevant to today's problems.

D. 1. Some religions have millions of followers.
   2. The Muslim religion should speak out more against Islamic terrorism.
   3. If you are a Catholic, you must be a Christian.
   4. If you are a Buddhist, you cannot be a Christian.
   5. If you are Jewish, you must believe in a transcendent God.

E. 1. Any man who treats women merely as sexual objects is a male chauvinist.
   2. Sexual intercourse is copulation.
   3. Sex is immoral when its participants are irresponsible.
   4. One can't be a puritan and enjoy sex.
   5. Too much sex is abnormal.

F. 1. Democracy is a fragile form of government that is often put to the test.
   2. The true test of a democratic government is whether the majority of its citizens would be permitted to elect a dictator.
   3. If you don't believe in freedom, you don't believe in democracy.
   4. The real virtue of a democracy is that in the long run its leaders' mistakes are correctable.
   5. Capitalism has helped American democracy to survive.

What Is the Meaning of Key Terms?

Clarifying meaning is one of the philosopher's most important activities. Before you can determine the correctness or adequacy of a philosophical thesis, you must understand the thesis. It is impossible to determine the truth or falsity of a claim such as "Machines cannot be conscious," for example, until you ascertain just what 'being conscious' involves. In this section, we shall examine two of the most important methods of clarifying meaning: (1) presenting paradigm and borderline examples, and (2) developing adequate definitions.

Paradigm and Borderline Examples   Paradigm examples play a strategic role in clarifying meaning. They illustrate the essential meaning of concepts. Martin Luther King, Jr. is a paradigm of the concept of a nonviolent, black civil-rights leader, just as Albert Einstein is a paradigm of scientific genius and Christianity is a paradigm of religion. For any concept, there are usually a number of paradigm examples.

Paradigm examples often function as a point of departure for clarifying concepts. When asked to define 'justice' or 'intelligence', for example, many of us may be struck temporarily speechless. Rather than try to define them immediately, a helpful strategy is to cite a paradigm example and then to identify its essential characteristics. With these characteristics we can then build a good definition. For example, what is a 'moral prophet'? Jesus was certainly one. What essential characteristics of Jesus suggest classifying him as a moral prophet? Perhaps one characteristic is his advancing an effective and novel set of principles of good interpersonal relations: Love your neighbor, Turn the other cheek, Judge not lest you be judged. This characteristic, then, should be built into the definition of a 'moral prophet'.

Paradigm examples serve both as starting points for a definition and as anchoring points that will hold it firm. Implicit in the use of paradigms is the assumption "If case X is not an instance of concept Y, then I don't know what is!" An example might be "I don't know what your concept of pornography is, but it must include photographs of oral sex."

Now let's look at a second type of clarifying illustration: borderline examples. As their name suggests, borderline examples are used to clarify the limits of a concept's applicability. They are often helpful when, although we understand the essential meaning of a concept, we are uncertain how far that meaning extends. For instance, is Confucianism a religion? That is, does the term 'religion' describe Confucianism? Some writers have noted that Confucianism is almost exclusively concerned with social relations—reverence for authority, the family, and so on—and have concluded that it should not be classified as a religion. Confucianism seems to lack what other religions, such as Christianity and Judaism, have—namely, a conception of a divine being and our relation to this being. Thus Confucianism falls outside the limits of religion for those who hold that belief in a supreme being is an essential part of its definition. Of course, one may argue that Confucianism should be classified as a religion precisely because of its emphasis upon social relations and the proper conduct of life. Whichever way we decide, however, certain limits of applicability of 'religion' will be clarified, and the meaning of that concept will be understood to extend to those limits.

Borderline examples must sometimes be invented when no actual cases readily appear. Suppose that a strange drug were released into the earth's atmosphere and, as a result, things once perceived as green are now perceived as red. Does this imply that those same objects are now in reality red? What would the answer to this question tell us about our concepts of color and perception? Could we infer that if enough people merely *agree* about what they see, they know what they see? Or suppose the change were gradual. Would there come a point when we could no longer say we knew whether those objects were green or red? The purpose of raising such hypothetical situations is not merely to stimulate our imaginations; rather, it is to exercise our intellects in clarifying meaning.

To clarify meaning by giving examples is to present what is called a **denotative** definition. Thus a denotative definition of 'democracy' would be America, France, Britain, Australia, and so forth. Paradigm and borderline examples are simply types of denotative definitions. By contrast, a **connotative** definition presents properties that something must have in order to belong to a certain class. For example, something must have the property of three-sidedness to belong to the class of triangles. From here on, when we talk about definitions we shall mean connotative definitions.

Testing Definitions Turning, then, to our second strategy for clarifying meaning, how does one go about examining a (connotative) definition? The answer to this question depends largely on determining the type of definition proposed. Although there are many different types of definitions, we shall focus on two in particular: reportive and reformative.

A *reportive definition* states the meaning (or meanings) of a concept as it is used in our language. It reports what is generally understood to be the meaning of the particular concept. A reportive definition of 'automobile' would be "four wheeled, motorized vehicle designed for the transportation of a few people over land." Dictionary entries are usually reportive. A definition may be reportive even if it expresses a technical or specialized sense that is commonly understood only by members of particular groups. For physicists, for example, 'neutrino' has an established reportive definition. Linguistic usage is a reasonably objective standard for testing the correctness of a reportive definition. To define 'tobacco' as "any substance that may be smoked," for example, is simply wrong. 'Tobacco' is not alone in being used in this way. As every student knows, other substances may be smoked.

In defining a concept, one states the essential characteristics that something must have in order to be an example of the concept. For example, the properties of being male and unmarried must be possessed by any person who is a bachelor. These properties must accordingly be incorporated within a definition of 'bachelor'. In stating a concept's essential characteristics, one establishes limits of its applicability. These limits are found by determining that the concept and its reported meaning both fit the same cases. If they do not, then the proposed definition should be changed. For example, if "one who attends church regularly" were an adequate definition of 'moral person', then all people we describe as moral would be churchgoers and all churchgoers would be described as moral. But this is not the case since there are both immoral churchgoers and moral nonchurchgoers.

There is a very simple technique for evaluating the correctness of reportive definitions—the method of counterexample. A *counterexample* is a fact that allegedly falsifies a certain claim, in this case, a definitional claim. Consider the thesis that 'love' means "emotional involvement". Is there any person we could describe as in love yet not in some way emotionally attached? Probably not. There seem to be no counterexamples to the thesis that if a person is in love, then he or she is also emotionally attached. Anyone in love falls within the class of those emotionally attached in some way.

That there is no counterexample, however, to the thesis that love always incorporates emotional involvement does not prove that the thesis is an adequate definition. Counterexamples work in *two* directions, and if the thesis is an adequate definition, then there must also be no counterexample to its converse, that 'emotional involvement' means 'love'. Now, some persons do not love the person or thing they are emotionally attached to. One individual may be emotionally dependent on another, for instance, yet be totally insensitive to his or her needs and lack all respect. There is therefore a counterexample to the thesis that if a person is emotionally attached, then he or she is in love. 'Being in love' and 'being emotionally attached' need not apply to the same class of persons. The conceptual limits in question do not coincide; rather, one concept "contains" the other. This is illustrated in the scheme in Figure 4.1.

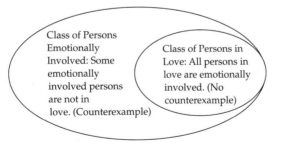

'Love' ◄— means? —► 'emotionally involved'

Class of Persons Emotionally Involved: Some emotionally involved persons are not in love. (Counterexample)

Class of Persons in Love: All persons in love are emotionally involved. (No counterexample)

Figure 4.1 In an adequate definition there would be no counterexamples and the two circles would coincide. This definition is both too narrow, because more is involved in love than just emotional attachment, and too broad, because "emotional involvement" can include negative feelings, such as fearfulness, too.

When there are counterexamples, the definition is said to be *too broad* or *too narrow* or both.

The use of counterexamples is reasonably objective insofar as it is based on empirical facts. Indeed, this is one of the most common ways empirical data figure in philosophical investigation. 'Love' is taken to mean more than "emotional involvement." Reportive definitions must remain true to those facts. When we come to reformative definitions, however, we shall see that the picture changes considerably.

Reformative definitions are intended to improve upon existing definitions, to be better explanations of the meaning of the concept in question. Their advocates are less concerned with what others may understand than with the truth of the matter. Be prepared for a reformative definition when you hear someone announce, "I'm going to tell you what love really is." Reformative definitions are profound and interesting, yet troublesome, proposals in philosophy. How should they be evaluated? Although reformative definitions can be arbitrary, they usually are not in philosophy. Often they conform partially to common meanings with which we are already familiar. To this extent, they may, like reportive definitions, be evaluated along empirical lines. The definition's more provocative aspect, however, must be examined in light of the reasons that are advanced for it.

Reformative definitions sometimes emphasize one established meaning in preference to others. Thus it may be argued that the essential nature of love is respect, not passion or understanding. Often, however, they bring to the surface meanings we had just never thought of before. To make these meanings more plausible, competing definitions may be examined and rejected in the process. This is the strategy Plato uses in many of his dialogues.

In his *Republic,* for example, he answers the questions "What is justice?" and its more specific variation "What is a just individual?" He defines a just individual as a virtuous individual and then proceeds to define virtue as the fulfillment and harmonious function of our rational, emotional, and biological natures, according to the type of persons we are. Since a fulfilled and well-balanced person is happy, it follows that happiness is part of the nature of justice—that being just or virtuous is its own reward. To establish this definition, Plato offers a variety of arguments through Socrates, who is his mouthpiece in the dialogue. Socrates is portrayed as arguing, for example, that the popular definition of justice as whatever is in the interests of the stronger (a variation of the thesis "Might makes right") is self-refuting. For those in power ultimately work against their own real interests. The tyrant who manipulates his subjects cannot be happy, and hence cannot be just, because he is "unbalanced," that is, he is overcome with fear and greed. Plato marshals his arguments and directs them to persuading us that his conception is what justice must have been all along.

We cannot explore the subtleties of Plato's various arguments here. The important point to notice about reformative definitions is this: If you do not agree with a certain definition, your strategy should not be to insist, "I don't choose to define it that way." Nor should it be simply to appeal to some commonly accepted definition, for that definition is precisely the point at issue. Rather, you should examine the arguments Plato or any philosopher advances in support of reforming the meanings of a term.

A word of caution about reportive and reformative definitions is necessary. You should be on guard against making a definition true by decree; that is, you should not refuse to recognize when counterexamples or arguments may count against it. A simple example of this fallacy is found in the repeated insistence that a person is not really "religious" unless he or she worships a supreme being. Partially correct, this definition suffers from arbitrariness in view of numerous counterexamples. For example, Buddhists do not worship a supreme being.

Another example of the fallacy is found in discussions of what counts as a "liberated" woman. Some feminists, for example, may argue for the following reportive–reformative definition: A woman is liberated only if (1) she is realizing her potential as a person, (2) she is defining her own values, and (3) those values do not reflect the interest of male dominance. Others may point out, however, that the third condition is too restrictive because there are liberated women who satisfy the first and second conditions and are happy as sex objects and homemakers. This criticism, however, may meet with the counterargument that any woman who is happy or satisfied with these roles has simply not escaped the brainwashing of a male-dominated culture.

This counterargument sometimes carries a degree of arbitrariness that infects the definition of 'liberated woman'. The arbitrariness emerges in the following way. Take the case of Linda, who is intelligent, morally sensitive, and politically aware, and who points out that she knows the difference between being brainwashed and choosing to subordinate certain of her interests to those of her husband. Her more radical sisters then argue that if she is satisfied with this relatively subordinate position, then she must be brainwashed and cannot be "really" liberated. In effect, restrictions are placed by decree over which values Linda can define for herself. Counterexamples for a sizeable number of women are ruled out in advance. This procedure should always be avoided in philosophy when you are attempting to develop an adequate reportive or reformative definition.

Exercises

Evaluate the following definitions by citing counterexamples:

A. A psychic is one who knows your future.
B. Morality is what most persons feel is moral.

    C. A cause is any event that regularly precedes another event.

    D. A philosophical problem is a problem for which science has not yet found the answer.

    E. Virtue is nothing other than happiness.

    F. A good teacher is one who knows the subject well.

    G. Knowing something just means believing it sincerely and strongly.

    H. A true belief is one that works.

    I. Justice is paying off one's friends and punishing one's enemies.

    J. Love is respect.

    K. A lie is a misstatement.

    L. Feminists want only equality between the sexes.

    M. An unidentified flying object (UFO) is a spaceship that has come from another world.

V
Doing Philosophy:
Further Considerations

The tools surveyed in Chapter IV should help us get started in the effort of philosophical analysis. They help us "size up" the territory, identify the problem(s), and make certain that we understand what is at stake. Having performed some of these preliminary operations, it remains for us to get down to business, so to speak, and determine just what can be said both for and against a theory in question. In addition to the individual sets of exercises at the end of each section, there are two case studies at the end of this chapter that pull together all of the techniques in analyzing a single issue.

Do the Arguments
Support the Thesis?

Recognizing the Argument Arguments are composed of statements, one of which (the conclusion) allegedly follows from the others (premises).[1] Statements may be defined as true or false sentences. Unfortunately, many arguments are not stated in a clear, one-two-three fashion. The conclusion, for example, may be both preceded and followed by supporting premises in a jumbled manner; the conclusion is not

---

[1]A debated exception to this general rule is an "imperative" argument, in which a moral prescription appears in both a premise and conclusion. An example is "Never tell lies (premise); this would be a lie (premise); so don't say this (conclusion)."

always presented at the end of an argument. To distinguish between the premises and conclusion, it is helpful to keep in mind that expressions such as "since," "because," and "in view of" usually introduce premises, and expressions such as "hence," "therefore," and "it follows that" usually introduce the conclusion.

Just because you may spot one of these expressions, however, don't think that what follows is always a premise or a conclusion. For example, the sentence "Since you didn't heed my warnings, I therefore order you to cease" does not express an argument at all. Why not? To begin with, the second clause, which perhaps looks like a conclusion, is not a statement about what is the case; it is a command. (Commands may be just or unjust, but they are neither true nor false.) And arguments are composed entirely of (true or false) statements, not of commands, questions, or exclamations. In addition, the first clause, which perhaps looks like a premise, is not *evidence* for the truth of "I therefore order you to cease." Instead it expresses a brief *explanation* of why the command is being given. The premise of an argument should provide a reason for believing the conclusion to be so.

Once you have ascertained that an argument is advanced and have distinguished between the premises and conclusion, it is often helpful to take the relevant statements from their context—perhaps rewrite them more clearly and concisely—and arrange them so that the premises precede the conclusion. As an example, the following passage expresses an argument very similar to one advanced by the philosopher René Descartes (1596–1650): "I cannot be identical with my body, since if I were, both my existence and my body's existence would be equally doubtable, and they are not." Here it is rewritten in its proper form:

1. If I am identical with my body, then my existence and my body's existence should be equally doubtable.
2. But my existence and my body's existence are not equally doubtable.

---

3. Therefore, I am not identical with my body.

This argument is deductive in form. A **deductive** argument is one in which it is claimed that the conclusion is necessarily implied by the premises. If a deductive argument is valid, there is a necessary connection between the premises and conclusion; the conclusion necessarily follows from the premises. An **inductive** argument, in contrast, is one in which it is claimed that if the premises are true, they give only a certain degree of probability to the conclusion. The following is a simple example: "Heart trouble occurs more frequently among smokers than among nonsmokers, so that smoking (probably) contributes to heart trouble." No matter how true or complete the evidence expressed by the premises, there always exists a contingent connection between the premises and the conclusion of an inductive argument. That is, given true premises, the conclusion doesn't necessarily follow.

Induction: Testing Analogical Arguments There are many types of inductive arguments that conform to the general description just given. We shall focus, however, on one very important type called *analogical* arguments, which are found in many everyday inferences as well as in philosophical arguments. For example, I like most of the science-fiction works by a certain author and conclude that I will probably like that author's latest science-fiction piece. Arguments for the probable existence of life on other planets are analogical, based upon presumed similarities between conditions on earth and conditions on other planets. Analogical arguments proceed from the similarities of two or more things in certain respects to their similarity in some additional respect. They have the following common form:

1. Items A, B, and C have characteristics x and y.
2. A and B have characteristic z.

3. Therefore, C probably has characteristic z also.

A very widely discussed argument in philosophy with this form is an inductive proof of the existence of God called the "argument from design" (or sometimes the "teleological argument for the existence of God"). A writer named William Paley (1743–1805) reasoned as follows. The world and pocket watches have a number of common properties. For example, the efficient functioning of the whole is dependent upon the proper functioning of the parts, and the many parts often stand in a delicate balance to each other. Watches are created by human intelligence. Therefore, the world must have been designed and created by an intelligence far superior to ours, namely, God.

The relative strength or weakness of an analogical argument depends upon several factors:

1. The number of samples used—the more the better, up to a point
2. The number and variety of characteristics that appear to be similar in the samples
3. The strength of the conclusion relative to the premises
4. The relevance of the characteristics cited in premises to the conclusion drawn
5. The number of differences among the samples cited in the premises—usually, the greater the number, the stronger the conclusion
6. The number of differences between the samples cited in the premises and the instance cited in the conclusion—usually, the greater the number, the weaker the conclusion

Inductive arguments are weaker or stronger by degree; they needn't be accepted or rejected on an "all-or-nothing" basis. Unlike deductive arguments, they are never said to be valid or invalid.[2]

Consider some examples. The third of our six factors has been adduced by critics of the "argument from design." They argue that, even if the order and balance of nature were to prove the existence of a cosmic designer, it would not prove the existence of a perfect personal being, God, since there are many imperfections in the world. A conclusion asserting the existence of such a being would be too strong for the premises. To take a different example, the fifth and sixth factors are often relevant in classifying certain actions as right or wrong. That breaking one's promise is wrong in most situations might tempt you to conclude that breaking one's promise would also be wrong in the present situation. The strength of this conclusion would depend largely upon whether there are any crucial differences between the usual situation and your present situation. Suppose they did not involve saving a life, whereas this one does; you need to break a promise to save a life. If so, you would conclude that in this particular case promise breaking is right. It is right because of the dissimilarity between the usual cases and your present, special situation.

Deduction: Testing for Validity   Let's now get back to the topics of deduction and validity. You may be accustomed to using the term 'valid' to mean 'true', as in the phrase "a valid point of view." But in logic and philosophy validity has a different sense. Validity concerns the structure or form of a deductive argument, not the truth or falsity of the individual premises and conclusions. A valid argument can have false premises and/or a false conclusion, but never true premises and a false conclusion. One way to determine the validity of a supporting argument, therefore, is to see whether it possesses a valid argument form. A few common forms with their standard "labels" are as follows:

Modus Ponens	Modus Tollens	Hypothetical Syllogism	Disjunctive Syllogism
If p then q (or p implies q) p	If p then q (or p entails q) Not q	If p then q If q then r	Either p or q Not p
Therefore, q	Hence, not p	Hence, if p then r	Therefore, q

In each of these argument forms p, q, and r are arbitrarily chosen letters that stand for simple sentences. No matter what we substitute for p, q, or r, the resulting argument will be valid. For instance, in the first

---

[2]A more extensive treatment of analogical arguments appears in Irving Copi's *Introduction to Logic*, 6th ed. (New York: Macmillan, 1982), pp. 232–35.

form, modus ponens, we might substitute "Fetuses are persons" for p and "Abortion is murder" for q. The result would be

1. If fetuses are persons (p), then abortion is murder (q).
2. Fetuses are persons (p).

---

3. Therefore, abortion is murder (q).

The premises and conclusion may be false (that is a different problem), but the argument form is valid. Here is another example of a valid form of argument, this time in the form called hypothetical syllogism:

1. If there are quotas for enrolling minority groups in colleges and universities (p), there will soon be quotas for graduating minorities, too (q).
2. If there are quotas for graduating minorities (q), then academic standards will go down (r).

---

3. Therefore, if there are quotas for enrolling minority groups (p), then academic standards will go down (r).

Associated with each of the above four valid argument forms are four additional forms that, although they may appear valid, are actually invalid. These common invalid forms are as follows:

Affirming the Consequent	Denying the Antecedent	Hypothetical Fallacy	Affirming the (inconclusive) Disjunct
If p then q	If p then q	If p then q	Either p or q
q	Not p	If p then r	p
---	---	---	---
Therefore, p	Therefore, not q	Hence, if q then r	Hence, not q

Suppose we let p represent "You study" and q "You'll pass the final." Affirming the consequent in the first form produces an invalid argument because there are other ways of passing the final than studying. Because you pass the final doesn't mean that you studied for it. You could have already mastered all the necessary information. The same explanation applies to the fallacy of denying the antecedent in the second invalid form. Just because you don't study doesn't mean you won't pass the final. You might pass it on luck alone. In the third form, let us add "You'll graduate" for r. This form now says merely that your passing the final ensures your graduation just because you have studied, which clearly does not follow.

For practice, and to help make the fallacious nature of the fourth invalid form more clear, let us substitute "John inherited a lot of money" for *p* and "He won a sweepstakes" for *q*. This fallacious argument now affirms that because John either inherited a lot of money or won the sweepstakes, and because he in fact inherited a lot of money, then we may conclude that he didn't win the sweepstakes. However, this conclusion does not validly follow because both disjuncts in the first premise could be true. Inheriting a lot of money does not in itself rule out winning a sweepstakes, too. The fallacy occurs because of the *inclusive* sense of "or," which allows both disjuncts to be true. If the disjuncts were *exclusive*, as in "Either John is a U.S. president, or he is a German citizen," the argument would have been valid since if he's one he cannot be the other.

The foregoing argument forms illustrate inferences drawn from the relations between simple sentences. A different kind of deductive reasoning consists in drawing inferences from *class membership*. This type of reasoning was first discussed and organized by Aristotle. Class membership may be affirmed (partly or wholly) or denied (partly or wholly). These possibilities may be combined to give us a relatively large number of argument forms. A few are

| All *p* is *s* | No *s* is *p* | All *p* is *r* | Some *s* is not *r* |
No *r* is *s*	Some *r* is *p*	Some *s* is *p*	All *p* is *r*
No *r* is *p*	Some *r* is not *s*	Some *s* is *r*	Some *s* is not *p*

In these argument forms, *p*, *r*, and *s* denote classes, such as people with red hair, democrats, true believers, toads, or revolutionaries—whatever classes happen to be in question. For example, if *p*, *r*, and *s* stand for true believers, democrats, and revolutionaries, then we may construct the following valid argument:

1. All true believers (*p*) are revolutionaries (*s*).
2. No democrats (*r*) are revolutionaries (*s*).

3. Therefore, no democrats (*r*) are true believers (*p*).

Again, you may question the truth of the individual statements, but the inference from the premises to the conclusion is valid.

There are hundreds of valid as well as invalid argument forms that, short of undertaking a course in logic, we cannot begin to survey. Indeed, we have not even begun to scratch the surface of the many interesting topics in logic. But a general rule of thumb will enable you to test a deductive argument for its validity without having to rely on the formal proof procedures you would learn in a logic course. This rule is based on the definition of validity and involves the use of counterexamples. A valid argument is one such that if the premises are true, then the conclusion must also be true. Alternatively, if the argument is valid, it cannot have all true premises and a false conclusion. If the premises themselves are true and the conclusion is false, the argument must be invalid, for a false conclusion cannot be validly deduced from true premises. So, if you can imagine circumstances in which the premises could be true and the conclusion false, then you will have proved the argument in question invalid. Consider our earlier example:

1. If you study, you'll pass the final.
2. But you can't study.

---

3. So you won't pass the final.

It is possible that both of the premises are true here, and that you do pass the final, perhaps by cheating or guessing. In this case the original conclusion would be false. You may happen to fail the exam. But in deductive arguments, the claim is that if the premises are true and the inference valid, you must fail the exam. If it is even possible that the premises are true and the conclusion false, the argument is invalid.

Consider a different deductive inference, this one based on class membership:

1. All Muslims support terrorism.
2. Bill is a Muslim.

---

3. Therefore, Bill supports terrorism.

In this argument, both the premises and the conclusion happen to be false. The inference itself, however, is valid. Why? Well, suppose the premises were true. Could you think of a counterexample to the conclusion—something that would falsify Bill's supporting terrorism—if those premises were true? No, you could not. (Try it and see!) If the premises are presumed true and there are no possible counterexamples to the conclusion, the argument is valid, whereas if there are some possible counterexamples, the argument is invalid.

Exercises

Test the validity of the following arguments by the method of counterexample or by comparison with a valid argument form. (Note: Some arguments may not fit the few forms discussed in this chapter.)

A. 1. If all people are equal, then all should have the same rights.
    2. All people are not equal.

    ---

    3. Therefore, all people should not have the same rights.

B. **1.** If time is identical with physical change, then time stops when physical change stops.
    2. If time stops when physical change stops, then it should not make sense to ask: "For how long did physical change cease?"
    3. But it does make sense to ask this question.

    4. Therefore, time is not identical with physical change.

C. **1.** If philosophy is many things to many people, there should be much confusion over what philosophy is.
    2. There is much confusion over what philosophy is.

    3. Therefore, philosophy is many things to many people.

D. **1.** Either AIDS represents a covert depopulation policy or it does not.
    2. If it does, then we cannot trust our government.
    3. But we must trust our government.

    4. Therefore, AIDS does not represent a covert depopulation policy.

E. **1.** If Jones's argument has all true premises and a false conclusion, then it is invalid.
    2. Jones's argument has all true premises and a false conclusion.

    3. Therefore, Jones's argument is invalid.

F. **1.** Some biologists believe that mothers with large families should be sterilized.
    2. All defenders of civil liberties reject that belief.

    3. Hence, no defenders of civil liberties are biologists.

Are the Premises True?

Before discussing the truth of the premises, we need to touch briefly on the topic of soundness. A deductive argument is said to be sound only if it is valid and its premises are true. Like validity, soundness is a potential characteristic of the argument as a whole. To be precise, there are neither valid premises or conclusions nor sound premises or conclusions. It is only an argument that may be sound. If a deductive argument has either false premises or an invalid inference, it is unsound and should be rejected. Soundness never applies to inductive arguments because, as you recall, they are neither valid nor invalid, and soundness involves truth and validity.

We have just seen how to test the validity of a deductive argument. To determine the argument's soundness, you also need to check the truth of the premises. Most philosophical arguments contain one or more empirical premises that can be checked by observation and science. Most of your efforts will be directed to determining the truth of the nonempirical premises (and every philosophical argument, you recall, has at least one). Moreover, how you go about examining the truth of these premises will depend upon what kind of nonempirical claim is made. Is it presented as a self-evident synthetic a priori claim, for example, one that asserts a necessary connection between freedom and responsibility? Is it a reformative definition? Moreover, there are other critical questions you may wish to apply to the nonempirical premises as well as to general philosophical beliefs and theories. We shall discuss them in the following sections.

Are the Assumptions Correct?

To examine the role of assumptions in philosophical investigation, we need to make the distinction between **necessary** and **sufficient conditions** explicit. A condition is necessary if it must be the case in order for a certain belief to be true or for a certain event to occur. Without this condition, the belief would not be true or the event would not occur. For example, John's being unmarried is necessary for "John is a bachelor" to be true. Or, fuel is necessary for combustion. A condition is sufficient when, if it is the case, it follows that a certain belief is true or a certain event will occur. Thus, John's being unmarried is not sufficient for the truth of "John is a bachelor." But John's being unmarried and his being a male are together sufficient for the truth of that claim. Similarly, if fuel, oxygen, and ignition obtain, then combustion follows. Of course, philosophers are not particularly interested in necessary or sufficient conditions viewed as causes of natural events. That is the scientist's area. They are interested, however, in necessary or sufficient conditions insofar as they imply *logical* connections between beliefs. Let us see how.

The Roles of Necessary and Sufficient Assumptions
A philosophical theory or thesis may have assumptions in either or both of two senses. First, an assumption may operate as a necessary condition of a certain theory. Second, it may operate as a sufficient condition of a certain theory. It is important to determine which sense is in question because this will influence the effectiveness of questioning the theory's assumptions. We shall discuss both senses and make clear their relevance for critically analyzing a philosophical thesis.

When assumptions, taken singly or collectively, are a sufficient condition for a certain belief, then we say that they *entail* that belief. That is, given the assumption, the belief in question logically follows. If the assumption is true, then so is the belief. For example, if one accepts a **Marxist** economic theory, then this is in itself sufficient to reject the basic principles of capitalism. To be more specific, if one assumes that Marxist economic theory is true, then it follows that one believes that prices are not determined by a free-market interaction of supply and demand.

Now, questioning a theory's sufficient assumptions is not necessarily an effective means of disproving that theory. To return to our preceding example, suppose that you wish, by questioning Marxian assumptions, to disprove the theory that capitalism ought to be rejected. Suppose that you do succeed in showing that Marxist economic theory is itself false. What then? That Marxism might be wrong does not prove that prices are or should be determined by supply and demand. There are a variety of objections that might be raised against capitalism that are independent of Marxian economic theory—for example, that it may favor monopoly control of supplies. One does not have to be a Marxist to criticize capitalism. Thus, questioning this or any assumption that serves as a sufficient condition of a certain theory will not necessarily be effective. Even if you are successful, that theory still may or may not be true.

A more powerful and direct strategy is to attack those assumptions that are necessary conditions of the theory in question. Such assumptions are called *presuppositions.* Necessary conditions of a theory must be correct in order for the theory itself to be correct. The theory cannot be true if its presuppositions are not true. Necessary assumptions are said to be entailed by the theory they presuppose. Thus, if you can show them to be false, you will have directly refuted the theory you are questioning. (If you can show that they are true, however, you still have not shown that the theory itself is true.)

Questioning the presuppositions of a theory may involve the *modus tollens* form of argument described earlier. This form begins with a hypothetical premise ("If *p* then *q*"). This premise expresses the logical relation between the theory (*p*) and its assumption (*q*). The rejection of the assumption is expressed by the second premise ("Not *q*"), and your rejection of the theory follows in the conclusion ("Not *p*"). For example, suppose you wish to question the thesis that continuous economic growth is desirable. What is one of its presuppositions? One would be that natural resources are for all practical purposes inexhaustible. This is a dubious assumption. Your overall strategy takes the following form:

1. If continuous economic growth is desirable, then our natural resources must be practically inexhaustible.
2. But our natural resources are not inexhaustible.

---

3. Therefore, continuous economic growth is not desirable.

You may have noticed that this argument has a feature that perhaps does not square with an important point made in Chapter I. It looks as though we have just falsified a nonempirical claim, namely, a value judgment ("Continuous economic growth is desirable"), with a simple empirical fact ("Natural resources are not inexhaustible"). This does happen on a few occasions. But when it does, it is only because there is an agreement about the meanings of certain key terms and about certain borderline claims that are difficult to classify as empirical or nonempirical. An advocate of continuous economic growth could respond with, "Look, I didn't mean just resources in the ground here on earth, but rather, I had in mind solar energy (good for another few billion years) and the resources on other planets and star systems that someday we shall be able to mine." Or that person might just insist that even though natural resources will run out in the next fifty years, it is still desirable for us to look out for ourselves and let our grandchildren worry about the problem. These responses may seem a little stretched. Yet they are fairly realistic ways to avoid having one's value judgment falsified by empirical facts. That these and other responses are often in the background makes philosophical arguments slippery to deal with. And this is why philosophical claims are not empirically falsifiable in the sense that they admit a clean-cut, absolute refutation.

You may have noticed that the emphasis of this section has been on identifying assumptions and determining how their falsity may affect the truth of a certain theory. We have not said much about actually showing the assumptions per se to be correct or incorrect. This is because once the assumptions are identified and placed within the context of a theory, questions about their truth or falsity often resolve themselves. If some questions persist, however, the truth or falsity of the assumptions will have to be determined in a way that recognizes the type of claims they involve. Are they empirical? Necessary? Definitional? Do they follow from other arguments? Or we may ask whether they are in themselves more or less plausible than competing assumptions. We may, for example, be unable to prove that other people have experiences, even though their brains and behavior are similar to our own; but it is more plausible to assume that they do than to try to question that assumption.

The Importance of Background Assumptions   Not all assumptions can be neatly categorized as necessary or sufficient. There are always borderline cases. Often, assumptions are hidden in the background and must be brought to the surface by critical dialogue. Indeed, such dialogue is often the only means of determining the exact role that certain assumptions play in a theory. Consider the following claim: "Ceasing to require a morning recitation of the Lord's Prayer in public schools is 'antireligion'." Three possible assumptions of this claim are (1) that 'religion' means 'Christianity', to which the Lord's Prayer is uniquely tied, (2) that being religious means believing in a superior being, and (3) that religious education is best served by public communal expressions of prayer. The first and second assumptions can be classed as necessary, whereas the third probably comes close to being a sufficient assumption. Without further clarification, the issue is certainly debatable. But no matter what the assumptions of a theory may be or what their exact role is, disproving the assumptions will generally undermine the theory, and questioning them is always a sound critical strategy.

Evaluating assumptions is one of the primary tasks of philosophy, partly because we wish to avoid committing ourselves to views that rest on false assumptions. Furthermore, knowledge of shared assumptions is often essential to making positive advances in philosophical discussion. (Recall our discussion of "good movies" in Chapter I.) Implicit in our judgments are certain principles and ideals—assumptions that provide a standard with which to evaluate judgments. We judge according to our ideological commitments, whether they be to Christianity, conservatism, humanism, or astrology. For example, two Christians who assume that the Bible is the revealed word of God may use that belief as a standard in deciding whether salvation is attainable through good works alone. They may not ultimately agree, but at least their use of a common standard favors the possibility of agreement. In the absence of such a standard, the possibility of agreement is more remote. For example, how might a Christian attempt to "save" a Buddhist? If the attempt is based only on citation of the scriptures, chances are that it will fail. If the Buddhist and the Christian are to have a meaningful dialogue, they must isolate certain common assumptions. One such assumption might be that religious commitment should increase one's happiness and peace of mind. Given this assumption, the Buddhist and the Christian might then go on to discuss how following Jesus or Buddha leads to greater happiness. Similarly, in philosophy, determining common assumptions is an important condition of progress.

Exercises

On what potentially questionable assumptions do the following passages appear to rest?

A. If Congress would just pass more social legislation, we could eliminate crime.

B. President Obama is not a legitimate president because he is not a natural-born citizen.

C. If you are old enough to fight for your country, you are old enough to vote.

D. Abortions are perfectly moral because women have a right to control their own bodies.

E. Neuroscientists have correlated many brain states with experiences; the mind and the brain are therefore the same thing.
F. Judaism must be a true religion, for it has stood the test of time.
G. Those who have not served in the military should not be allowed to criticize publicly its rules and regulations.
H. Science has shown religion to be false.
I. If you don't vote, you don't count.
J. Of course Truman's decision to use nuclear weapons was justified—think of the lives it saved!
K. Because the dominant age-group of Americans is over fifty years, government policies ought to reflect the values of that age-group.
L. If there are genuinely free acts, then a science of human behavior is impossible.
M. New technology in genetics will soon allow us to have physically perfect children.

Are the Logical Consequences Plausible?

Another way to evaluate a philosophical theory is to determine whether it has logical consequences or implications that are themselves objectionable. If the consequences are objectionable, then the original thesis is weakened. The *modus tollens* form of argument again serves as a convenient means for evaluation. Suppose that someone claimed that whatever exists must be observable. Your response would take this form: "If this claim is correct, then what follows?" One consequence might be that consciousness must then not exist since it is unobservable. We might stop here with the conclusion that since consciousness obviously does exist then there must be something wrong with the initial thesis. Again, we could draw out a further logical implication such as this: "If consciousness does not exist, it follows that nobody is conscious, and (going still further) if nobody is conscious, then I must not be conscious as I think about this thesis. But this consequence is absurd; hence, there must be something wrong with the theory that whatever exists must be observable."

Moral philosophy offers many examples in which the consequences of a thesis figure very heavily in critical discussion. For example, what is implied by commitment to the "sacredness of life"? Is vegetarianism a logical consequence? Or preservation of the environment? Pacifism? Refusal to participate in experiments with our genetic code? (Remember Huxley's *Brave New World*?) Apathy? Why or why not? Would some of these possible logical consequences force us to qualify or even abandon the original principle?

The most unacceptable consequence of a theory is one that makes the theory self-defeating. A theory is self-defeating if it logically involves two or more claims that are inconsistent with each other. Here is an example. Philosophers called indeterminists defined a free action as an uncaused event because they believed that if all events were caused, there could be no free acts and thus no moral responsibility. Yet, they did want to preserve moral responsibility. To hold a person responsible, however, is to assume that a person has freely caused or brought about an act. Yet if the action was freely performed, it cannot have been caused, given the indeterminist definition of a free act. So, a logical consequence of this indeterminist definition of a free act is that persons cannot be held responsible for their actions. And this is inconsistent with a central tenet of indeterminism, namely, that persons can be held responsible for their acts. Hence the foregoing definition of freedom is self-defeating for the indeterminist theory. One cannot consistently deny what one implicitly assumes—a fallacy you should guard against in philosophical discussion.

Three Types of Consequence   Before moving on, we should clear up some possible confusion about the concept of consequences. Briefly, we should distinguish between the consequences of (1) an empirical hypothesis, (2) a valid deductive argument, and (3) a philosophical thesis. These consequences may be confused because they all involve hypothetical if-then inferences, but there the similarity begins to fade.

To begin with, the consequences of an empirical hypothesis take the form of predictions that certain events will (or did) occur under specified conditions. For example, if the earth is surrounded by a "sea of air," then a barometer's reading should decrease as it is taken to higher elevations. The consequences of deductive arguments and philosophical theses do not take this form.

The consequences of a valid deductive argument follow as a result of certain basic rules of inference (*modus ponens*, *modus tollens*, and so forth) and may have nothing to do with the real world at all. Deductive arguments are found in virtually all areas of inquiry; they are not peculiar to philosophy, science, religion, or any other discipline.

Finally, consider the consequences of a philosophical thesis. They, too, involve a hypothetical if-then inference, but although they may be described as "logical," they do not follow as the result of applying any rules of inference; rather, they follow directly from the thesis itself, usually because certain definitions or necessarily true propositions are involved. For example, it has been argued that if God is morally perfect, then He should not have created a world in which evil exists. In this claim there is an alleged incompatibility between God's moral perfection and anything even potentially evil. The assumption is that something potentially evil cannot in principle follow from something that is morally perfect.

An argument in which all three types of consequences are found is

1. If a government is truly representative, then it is responsive to the needs of the poor. (Alleged necessary, and analytic, consequence of the concept of a truly representative government)
2. If Smith is elected, the government will not be responsive to the needs of the poor. (Alleged empirical consequence of Smith's being elected)

---

3. Therefore, if Smith is elected, the government will not be truly representative.[3] (Deductive consequence)

Assumptions Versus Consequences: A Final Note   In Chapter I it was explained that, from a purely logical point of view, the necessary assumptions of a theory are indistinguishable from the consequences that follow necessarily from that theory. Any theory logically implies both its own assumptions and its consequences. If *P* implies *Q*, then *Q* could be either a presupposition or a logical consequence of *P*. This can cause some difficulty in distinguishing a presupposition from a consequence. In fact, it might be argued that, so long as we recognize that there is some logical relationship between the theory and what it implies, it's not terribly important to distinguish between assumptions and consequences.

Still, this is a distinction that we make in everyday life and ordinary reasoning. So even if there are no hard and fast logical criteria that could make the distinction for us, there are still some psychological criteria or general rules of thumb that may help where common sense comes up short. Here are a few to consider.

1. A theory *depends* upon its assumptions but not upon its consequences. For example, consider the thesis that universities should allow students to set their own curricula. This thesis depends upon the assumption (among others) that students are mature enough to make such decisions. But its truth does not depend upon its consequences—for example, that there should be no required courses. If anything, we would say that the consequences depend upon the theory and the theory in turn depends upon its assumptions. So consider, first of all, which way the relations of dependence seem to be pointing.

---

[3]This valid argument involves rules of inference from an area of logic called quantificational logic, which we cannot discuss here.

2. A closely related rule of thumb is to consider the *temporal priority* it would be reasonable to assign the various elements. One normally makes the assumptions of a theory, whether consciously or not, before one makes one's theoretical claim or begins to think seriously about the consequences of that claim. You would never argue, for example, that universities should allow students to set their curricula if you didn't already believe that students are mature enough to make such decisions. The consequences are usually still waiting to be drawn out.

3. Finally, the assumptions of a theory are often, though not always, a little broader in scope than the particular consequences inferred from it. Consider the claim that philosophy is worthwhile only if it helps one get a job. A rather broad assumption of this claim is that money is more important than knowledge, which can apply to many areas of life. The consequence, "Check the want ads before you declare a major in philosophy," is much narrower in scope.

Exercises

Consider the logical consequences of the following statements. Do they make the statements questionable or self-refuting?

A. All generalizations are false.
B. Everyone should lie all of the time.
C. Depression is nothing but behaving in certain seemingly "depressed" ways.
D. One may define any word as one pleases.
E. If abortion really is murder, then _____.
F. If we could construct a robot that looked and behaved just like a regular person, we would still have no reason to believe that it is conscious.
G. Everyone ought to act only in self-interest.
H. Anything hazardous to health should be illegal.
I. Pornography should be censored.
J. In a democracy, what the majority votes for should be permitted.
K. We can know only our own experience.
L. If happiness is determined by success, and success is determined by money, then X must have been unsuccessful and unhappy.
M. The grass is always greener on the other side.
N. Everyone should be a nonconformist.
O. There is a rodeo on Saturday to support the Humane Society.

How Adequate Is the Theory?

The adequacy of a philosophical theory depends on how well it fits the cases to be interpreted.[4] The tightness of the fit is found by looking at potential counterexamples. If you can find examples that fit the theory although they should not, then the adequacy of the theory diminishes. Or if you can find cases that should fit the theory but do not, then its adequacy again diminishes.

Strategies in Examining Adequacy   Let's consider the first of our suggested strategies—that of citing examples that fit the theory but should not. Near the end of Chapter I we inferred from the claims that (1) 'good' means 'whatever is natural' and (2) sex is natural, that sex must therefore be good. But are all natural things 'good' things? When we look at this principle itself, it is inadequate because it justifies too much. For one thing, it entails that terminal cancer must be good because it is natural. Again, few of us would want to hold that San Francisco's being swallowed by an earthquake is good. Citing such counterexamples forces us to qualify the central principle as follows: Natural objects or events are good so long as nobody is hurt by them. This qualification helps, but the principle still needs further restriction. Sticks and mud, for example, are natural and in themselves hurt nobody. Yet it is not at all clear that we should call them "good" too.

The alternative strategy—that of citing examples that should fit the theory but do not—is encountered frequently in philosophical evaluation. Materialists such as Democritus (460–370 = B.C.) and Thomas Hobbes (1588–1679) claimed that everything except space and time is "reducible" to matter and motion. The difference between rocks and snakes, for example, is allegedly nothing more than a difference in the motion and position of atoms that constitute those objects. Hobbes even went so far as to define 'desire' as "motion toward" and 'aversion' as "motion away from." This may sound good at first. But a comprehensive theory of existence must account for everything that in fact exists—if it claims to be adequate. And it is hard to see how such things as electromagnetic energy, mental depression, and political values can be made to fit the categories of matter and motion. We observe the position of matter in space, for

---

[4]This is also true in science. But the adequacy of a scientific theory or law is usually judged according to its explanatory power, that is, its ability to generate accurate, testable consequences. And in this sense, explanatory power is not a criterion of adequacy for philosophical theories.

instance, but what sense would it make to measure the spatial position of a set of values? Again, mental depressions change, but do they move like material objects? The metaphysical theory that reality is reducible to the categories of matter and motion needs to be expanded to cover the kinds of existence we ascribe to the counterexamples cited earlier.

Inadequate theories often result from a narrow point of view at the outset. For example, it is said that Hobbes's materialism revealed a motion-intoxicated man. In generalizing from your personal experience, you should distinguish between relatively universal experiences, such as the feeling of pain, and experiences restricted to a smaller range of people, such as the feeling of leading a meaningless life. If you generalize from personal feeling to the thesis that life is meaningless, you face numerous counterexamples. Life just does not seem that way to many people. Similar restrictions apply to the still more individual claim "The mind must be distinct from the body because I've left my body on several occasions." Not only have the great majority of people not had a similar experience, but those who have would not necessarily interpret it as a case of actually leaving one's body. Generalizations based on personal experience should therefore be formulated with caution.

The use of counterexamples to test the adequacy of a philosophical theory appears again in certain criticisms of utilitarianism, as elaborated by Jeremy Bentham (1748–1832) and John Stuart Mill. Now, according to utilitarians of that school, an act is right to the extent that it maximizes total pleasure or happiness, and wrong to the extent that it does not. In choosing between alternative actions, one's obligation is to promote "the greatest happiness for the greatest number of people." Truman's decision to use nuclear weapons is one that appealed to an essentially utilitarian moral standard: It is preferable to take a large number of lives now in order to save an even greater number of lives later.

Although utilitarianism fits nicely with some of our moral intuitions, it is also subject to some important counterexamples. Specifically, there can be many occasions when an act that produces the most happiness is not one we would describe as "right": stealing money when the other fellow would not miss it and you need it; giving a prisoner to a lynch mob to avoid endangering others' lives and property; breaking your promise if, without harm to anyone, you can thereby further your career. In the light of such objections, many utilitarians have admitted that the original moral standard needs to be qualified. It should be emphasized that these counterexamples do not literally disprove or refute the utilitarian standard. Rather, they suggest the need to increase its adequacy—to make it applicable just to those cases in which it should be applicable.

A Special Case   You will often find philosophical theories that take the following form: What appear to be instances of one category are really instances of another category.[5] That is, what many people classify one way ought to be classified in a different way. Here are some examples: "Material objects are nothing but collections of sense-data"; "Objective values are all really subjective"; "There are no natural rights; rather, we possess only those rights we claim and defend"; "Persons who think they have seen ghosts were really just hallucinating." Philosophers who have made such claims are well aware that there are apparent counterexamples to their views. They generally believe, however, that they have good reasons for ruling out those counterexamples—for supposing that they are not genuine exceptions after all. So your citing such counterexamples will often not be very effective, and you will have to go directly to the supporting arguments themselves.

A good example of this special kind of claim is given by Plato. Plato had a rather low opinion of sense perception and held that the objects of knowledge were "forms" of pure ideas ('justice', 'greenness', 'smallness'), outside space and time. He classified claims such as "I know he hit the dog because I saw him do it" as mere beliefs, not knowledge. Plato had reasons for doing this. First of all, he pointed out, our senses often deceive us, and we can never be certain on any given occasion that we are not deceived. Moreover, since knowledge must involve true claims and truth must be unchanging, knowledge cannot be based upon sense perception; for sense perception is unreliable and continuously changing. Hence, genuine knowledge must be of something other than the objects of sense perception—namely, the pure and unchanging "forms," which must be grasped by reason. If you insist at this point, "I know what I see despite what Plato says," you will not really penetrate the issue and will probably beg the question against Plato, a fallacy we shall discuss shortly. To get to the heart of the matter, you should examine Plato's arguments and assumptions. You might begin, for example, by questioning his requirement that knowledge be totally "absolute" and immune to the very possibility of error.

Exercises

Test the adequacy in the following statements by citing counterexamples.

A.   Where there is a will, there is also a way.
B.   Psychology is concerned exclusively with predicting behavior.

---

[5]A category is a heading under which things may be classified or to which they belong. A system of categories (moral, metaphysical, and so forth) is a way of dividing up and interpreting isolated cases. Philosophical categories are fundamental or ultimate classifications.

    C. The purpose of dramatic acting is to make the spectators identify with the characters.

    D. Sensory pleasure is the only real goal of life.

    E. Our current big government must cut spending and reduce taxes.

    F. The central difference between science and philosophy is that science concerns itself with the observable world only, and philosophy concerns itself with abstract, unobservable entities. (Remember the discussion in Chapter I.)

    G. One is not educated unless one is trained to cope with the cold, cruel world.

    H. Something is better than nothing.

    I. It is better to have loved and lost than never to have loved at all.

    J. If extraterrestrials exist, they would not be interested in coming to investigate an inferior species such as ourselves.

Five Common Informal Fallacies[6]

In addition to the formal fallacies in argument described earlier, there are many common informal fallacies. These are found in quite different contexts, for example, news media, talk radio shows, college textbooks, and dinner table conversation. There are also far more than we can describe in this brief section—enough, in fact, to fill small textbooks in logic! They are called "informal" because they have no connection with formal validity or invalidity per se, and partly because their relevance to any conclusions being asserted tends to be emotional or to depend upon tricks or misuse of language. Once detected, all undermine the believability of the thesis being argued. In this section we will examine five such common fallacies, although your instructor may wish to supplement this discussion with some additional fallacies.

Question-Begging Arguments An argument begs the question (or, to use the Latin name, commits the fallacy of *petitio principii*) when it assumes the truth (or falsity) of the very claim it is supposed to prove (or disprove). There are a variety of question-begging arguments in philosophy. We shall review two of the most important types: circular arguments and question-begging definitions.

Suppose one wants to argue that capital punishment should be required of all convicted drug dealers. There are many statements one

---

[6]This section on fallacies is authored by my colleague, Professor Grant Luckhardt.

might want to present as evidence for this claim, for example, "Drug use is a major social problem," "Capital punishment puts an end to drug dealing by the person convicted and killed," "Capital punishment is effective against would-be criminals," and so on. Notice that each of these premises differs from, and is presented in support of, the conclusion argued for. Evidence should be independent of and supportive of the conclusion for which it is presented. It would not be evidence in favor of capital punishment for convicted drug dealers to state either that capital punishment should be meted out for all convicted drug dealers or that the butternut tree is a close relative of the walnut. The first statement is the same as the conclusion for which it is purportedly evidence and is therefore not independent of it; the second statement does not support (or have anything to do with) the conclusion.

Circular arguments present evidence that is like the first of these two statements in that they are not independent of the conclusion they purportedly support. One way they may fail to be independent of the conclusion is, as we have just seen, to be the same statement as the conclusion. Few would argue in such a patently fallacious way as to say, "Capital punishment should be required, therefore capital punishment should be required." But by rephrasing the conclusion, it can be disguised as a premise, and the same effect can be achieved: "Capital punishment should be required of all convicted drug dealers because they should be given the death penalty." Or consider: "Clear-cutting should be allowed in national forests because the federal government should allow timber to be harvested nonselectively." Or: "Humans have no free will because humankind is not capable of choosing freely." In all these examples, the evidence for the conclusion is really just the same statement as the conclusion; that is, the conclusion depends argumentatively on itself. This is why such fallacious arguments are called circular.

A more subtle form of circular argument occurs when the conclusion does not depend on itself but depends on another, independent premise or premises, which depend(s) on the conclusion. Consider: "God exists because the Bible says He does, and the Bible is true because it is the revealed word of God." Here the conclusion "God exists" depends on "the Bible says He does." The problem with this argument is that this premise depends on the further premise that the Bible is true. And this, according to the argument, depends on the Bible being the revealed word of God. But in order for it to be the revealed word of God, there must be a God. And this is the conclusion. So, by a larger circle, we still have an argument in which the conclusion depends on itself.

Question-begging definitions ensure that a conclusion will be true by using definitions that rule out any other possibility. Suppose that Jones asserts that no true American could support a trade sanctions bill. Smith might try to question that claim by pointing out that

Adams, an American, does support such a bill. Jones might then assert that this just goes to show that Adams isn't really an American. By redefining 'American' to exclude those who support a trade sanctions bill, Jones has ensured that his original claim is true. In order to argue against that claim, Smith needs to point out that Jones has redefined the word 'American' to suit his purposes and so has used a question-begging definition.

The use of the words 'real' and 'true' is often a sign that a question-begging definition is being used. "The real issue is . . . ," "The true meaning of the word so-and-so is such and such," "The only serious issue before us is . . ." often are used when arguers wish to redefine the issue or a word for their own purposes. In such cases, the careful reader must resist this attempt and stop the discussion from going forward: "Wait, that's not the 'real' meaning of so-and-so. That's just the meaning you've chosen to assign to it so that you won't have to discuss this or that other troublesome issue."

Question-begging definitions can appear in more subtle forms in philosophical discussions. Psychological egoism is the view that persons are always selfish. When apparently unselfish actions, such as parents sacrificing their vacations so their children can go to college, are presented as counterevidence to this claim, the psychological egoist often resorts to the tactic of redefining 'selfish' so that the parents' actions are considered selfish. Doing this begs the question by employing a definition. Notice that by redefining words, almost any claim can be made true. Consider the argument: "There are no dogs in the world." Against counterevidence to this claim, the defense might be offered that Fido, Blackie, and all other dogs are not really dogs, since they don't have wings and can't fly. If having wings and being able to fly is made a requirement of being a dog, then it is true that there are no dogs. But the definition that restricts the class of dogs in this way must be brought into question.

Ad Hominem Fallacy The *ad hominem* (Latin for "to the man") fallacy directs attention away from evidence for the claim to the person making the claim. The social, political, religious, or other views of the person, or the person's character, personal background, or self-interest, is focused on in order to support or discredit the statement the person has made. "You shouldn't listen to what she says, because she's a Communist (or a something else)" is sometimes used to discredit a person's statement. But this works only if we assume that all Communists (or other group) are mistaken about all matters, which is, of course, false. When a person introduces such a premise into an argument, we must separate our personal feelings about political affiliations, race, sex, background, and so forth from the truth of the question at hand. Racism is no doubt objectionable, but our distaste for it does not make this argument sound: "This new view about the causes of acid rain is false because it has been put forth by a racist." Ad hominem arguments can be put forth to support a claim as well as to discredit it. But it is just as fallacious to argue, "This new view about the causes of acid rain is true because it has been put forth by an antiracist" as it was to argue in the former way.

One very tempting form of the ad hominem fallacy is to assume that if the consequences of a view are in the interest of the person advancing the view, then the view must be false. An example is "You can't believe a word of what Professor X says about raising professors' salaries. Of course she's in favor of raising their salaries because she's one of them." Professor X may very well benefit from the view she advocates, but that alone does not render her view false or her argument unsound. Whether or not professors' pay raises are a good idea is an issue that is independent of the self-interest of the person arguing for the idea. It is a false claim that persons advocating something in their own self-interest cannot have a correct view about an issue, even though the person using such an ad hominem argument assumes they cannot.

It is important to note that sometimes a person's self-interest, character, or personal background may be relevant to the question at issue. In these cases, it is not a logical mistake or fallacy to refer to his or her self-interest or character or background. Whether a nominee for the president's cabinet is an alcoholic, for example, may be a very important issue insofar as it pertains to job performance. And if someone states that she is morally opposed to gambling, it would support a charge of hypocrisy to note that she had a financial interest in a casino. What would be fallacious would be to assert that an alcoholic's views concerning beverage taxes must be false or that a gambler's arguments concerning the legalization of pari-mutuel betting must be unsound because of their personal histories.

Genetic Fallacy The *genetic fallacy* occurs whenever someone assesses the value of a view or practice on the basis of the origins (genesis) of the view or practice. "You're not going to eat cornflakes, are you? Don't you know that they were originally invented by a quack doctor as a cure for an imaginary sexual malady?" criticizes the value of eating cornflakes based on the cereal's origin. But where and why cornflakes arose have no bearing on whether they are a good food. Similarly, criticizing certain religious practices because they were originally based on false beliefs about hygiene, causality, or medicine does not speak to the current role and importance of those practices in a religion. Perhaps the beliefs or practices did arise for wrong reasons. This does not necessarily mean they are worthless now. Religion is sometimes criticized because of its allegedly superstitious or scientifically naive origins. But again, such criticisms fail to take into account the current import of religion. Psychiatry, surgery, and anesthesia may all have had dubious origins, but this does not mean that they have no value. The question of value should be answered independently of how and where and for what purposes such practices arose.

Straw Man In the fallacy of attacking a *straw man*, a critic replaces the original point with an extreme or exaggerated version of it. Since it is easier to criticize an extreme position, the critic proceeds to attack the new position rather than the old. Suppose, for example, someone advocates banning any first use of intercontinental ballistic missiles by the United States. An unscrupulous critic might respond by inventing a straw man to attack: "My opponent says that he wants the United States to outlaw all its intercontinental ballistic missiles. Since this would leave us with no retaliatory capability, this is a dangerous position." By replacing the original claim that first use should be banned with the more extreme claim that all use should be banned, the critic has made his or her own job easier. Sometimes the person making the original claim will fail to see that his or her claim has been distorted and will even try to defend the new claim introduced.

Philosophers sometimes use straw men quite consciously, knowing that a distorted view is easier to attack than the original; but more often they are unaware that the view they seek to criticize is different from the one originally advocated. In reading a philosopher's criticism of someone else's views, you must carefully examine the original views to make sure that they have not been misrepresented.

Slippery Slope *Slippery slope* arguments resemble straw man arguments insofar as both distort a view in order to attack it. But slippery slope arguments do so in a special way by falsely claiming that adopting a particular view or course of action will result in certain inevitable and undesirable consequences. Thus, a bank official opposed to a 1 percent increase in interest on customers' deposits might argue that such an increase would lead to an even greater increase next year, and an even greater one the year after that, and so forth. By putting the proposal of a 1 percent increase on a slippery slope, the official can make it appear much riskier than it actually is.

Notice that the fallacy of slippery slope occurs when someone falsely claims that a proposal will lead to undesirable consequences. If someone can show that in fact a proposal will have a bad result, then there is no fallacy. An old Arabic saying cautions against letting a camel's nose in one's tent, because soon the camel will follow. If there is no reason to think the camel will follow, then the fallacy of slippery slope has been committed when, on this basis, the camel's nose is not admitted. Phrases to look out for that are suggestive of a slippery slope fallacy include, "But that just leads to . . . ," "But what you've proposed will result in . . . ," "Next you'll be saying that . . . ."

There are two ways to defend against a slippery slope. The first is to show that the alleged undesirable consequence does not follow inevitably from the proposal. The second is to grant that it does but to deny that the consequence is undesirable. "So be it," one can respond to some consequences.

Exercises

Identify the fallacy most obviously committed in the following examples (of the five just described) and state how that fallacy is committed.

   A. There is no point in listening to President Obama's speech, because he is just another Democrat.
   B. Materialism, the view that humans are just like rocks and sand, must be false.
   C. Legalizing first-trimester abortions is just one step away from slaughtering orphans, so abortion should not be legalized.
   D. Cuba is not really a Communist country, since it is not aligned with China.
   E. Sally should be trusted because she says she's trustworthy, and she wouldn't say that if she couldn't be trusted.
   F. A person's strongest motive always determines his or her actions. If we wish to determine which of a person's motives are the strongest, we need only examine what that person does.
   G. First the bombing and advisers, then Special Ops personnel, then ground troops, and pretty soon we will have a full-scale ground war in Afghanistan just as we did in Vietnam. Therefore, we should never get militarily involved there.
   H. We shouldn't listen to arguments by patriots that the federal government is seeking to take all our guns away, since patriots support blowing up buildings like they did in Oklahoma.
   I. Wall Street investment bankers typically support the World Trade Organization, which is known as an environmentally unfriendly institution.

This concludes our overview of a few techniques of evaluation that you should find useful. As we noted at the outset, skill in applying these and other tools in philosophical contexts must be developed by practice. Working through the following samples of philosophical analysis will reinforce your understanding of the techniques discussed.

An Example of Philosophical
Analysis: Near-Death Experience

Most of you are at least vaguely familiar with a phenomenon that has come to be called "near-death experience" (or NDE).[7] Persons who have had this experience typically exhibited some of the symptoms of clinical death for a few minutes, such as cardiac arrest, but were then resuscitated. They recount that during this brief time they "floated" up out of their bodies, observed events in their environment, felt great peacefulness, found themselves moving through a void or mist toward a white light, in some instances "communicated" with spirits of friends and family, and then chose to return to life. Most report profound changes in their approach to life and in their attitudes about death. Such experiences seem to be on the rise and are being debated with more frequency in print and at the various professional meetings of psychologists and physicians. The whole area is ripe for logical examination.

Currently, the great weight of professional opinion favors the view that NDEs are nothing more than hallucinations and tricks of the brain. A typical argument in support of this theory might go as follows: "Most persons want to believe that they will not die with their bodies. When their brains undergo a sudden change in chemistry, such as occurs with oxygen deprivation, the deep-seated desire for survival is no doubt triggered in the form of fanciful dreams. To suppose that persons might literally be out of their bodies is contrary to all of medical science. NDEs can't be anything but hallucinations." In what follows, we shall analyze this argument by applying some of the logical techniques discussed in the preceding chapters.

What Type of Claim Is Advanced?   We should begin by distinguishing the main thesis ("NDEs can't be anything but hallucinations") from its two supporting arguments. This claim seems to be empirical. But what evidence could count against it? Skeptics are usually so certain that NDEs are hallucinations that they will not permit anything to count against this claim. Counterevidence tends to be explained away. If the claim is not falsifiable, then it cannot be empirical. It is instead a priori. Behind all of this the attitude is sometimes found that "this is so incredible that we cannot take seriously any alleged evidence for the reality of NDEs."

---

[7]Perhaps the most popular and accessible introduction to the field is Raymond Moody's *Life After Life* (Covington, Ga.: Mockingbird Books, 1975).

What Are the Meanings of Key Terms? There are many terms or phrases in the literature on NDEs that invite clarification, and not all are equally critical to a decision on the reality of NDEs. It is very difficult to define clinical or physical "death," but we do not have to tie this term down to understand NDEs or to examine related pro and con arguments. The question of meaning does seem critical, however, in the supporting argument that NDEs are contrary to all of medical science. Well, what is it about medical science that would rule out taking NDEs as objective or factual? The claim that medical science assumes **materialism** to be true is probably intended here. Hence, **dualistic** beliefs about a mind or spirit that can exist independently of the body are ruled out at the beginning. We should ask whether our understanding of medical science requires that materialism be true, or (more conservatively), whether it requires merely that medical science restrict itself to that part of a person that can be physically treated and observed, thus leaving dualism an open question.

Do the Arguments Support the Thesis? There are a number of possibilities here. Let us grant the premises of one of the supporting arguments, i.e., that we desire immortality and that this desire is activated by sudden chemical changes in the brain during an NDE. Does it follow that NDEs are hallucinations? No. There is never a necessary connection between the fact of desiring something and the "reality" of that something once we get it. Or stated another way, even if we knew the cause(s) of NDEs, we could not conclude necessarily that persons did not temporarily leave their bodies. We would merely know that, if persons left their bodies during an NDE, certain changes in brain chemistry would have to take place. When the premises of an argument are consistent with a certain conclusion and with the denial (opposite) of that conclusion, there is no valid argument.

Are the Premises True? Not only does the conclusion not validly follow, but the truth of the premises from which it is claimed to follow is questionable. For example, is it true that most persons desire immortality? Perhaps it was true in another age, but there are, no doubt, a good number of individuals today who would be horrified at the prospects of living forever. If this premise were true, then why have so many confirmed atheists, materialists, and general skeptics had NDEs? Certainly they neither want survival nor expect it. And concerning the premise about chemical changes in the brain, it is still at the stage of speculation. Such changes are known to take place in the physical process of dying, but anything distinctive that is correlated with just those persons having NDEs has not been discovered. Finally, regarding the premise stating that NDEs are contrary to medical science, the truth depends on what is meant by "medical science," as we discussed earlier.

Are the Assumptions Correct? Let's take a closer look at the claim that medical science and NDEs are incompatible, particularly the reports of out-of-body experiences. The claim, we noted, seems to rest on the assumption that medical science must embrace materialism rather than dualism. That may be questionable in itself, but let's push a bit further. Suppose medical science does (correctly) embrace materialism. Are materialism and out-of-body experiences necessarily incompatible? Not really. For a materialist could say: "What we call mind or spirit is simply a complex field of energy vibrating at frequencies current technology is unable to measure. Normally this field interacts with another field we call the physical body but it is capable of surviving independently. The difference between an observable body and an unobservable mind is only one of degree or complexity, depending upon the rates of vibration." To be sure, this would be an unusual form of materialism. But it would be materialism. Matter is energy. Thus we need not falsely assume that materialism and NDEs are necessarily incompatible.

Are the Logical Consequences Plausible? Suppose we take at face value the conclusion that NDEs are hallucinations. What logically follows? Well, one aspect of the term 'hallucination' is "an experience of something that is not real." But if we assume that part of what is experienced in NDEs is "real," that is, actually exists, and, moreover, can be shown empirically to be so, we would then have to conclude that NDEs to a certain extent are not hallucinations. (Note the very close connections between questions of meaning, logic, and empirical fact.) Now, in point of fact, some persons who have experienced NDEs have described in considerable detail actual events that took place.[8] If so, they cannot have been hallucinating. It would appear that some of the consequences of the main thesis are not plausible.

How Adequate Is the Theory? An adequate theory accounts for all of the facts that fall within its scope. To suppose that NDEs are hallucinations would not account for how some persons are able to accurately report specific events in an emergency or operating room. These are not hallucinations. Moreover, this theory would not explain how NDEs occur in the absence of significant brain wave activity, as in the case of "flat" EEGs (if one is hallucinating, there should be some brain wave activity). Therefore, the materialist theory that goes with the hallucination proposal is inadequate as it stands. However, it might be expanded along the lines suggested earlier to encompass a broader

[8]For a discussion of this evidence, see Michael Sabom, *Recollections of Death* (New York: Harper & Row, 1982).

range of data. To do so would not prove materialism true in any strict sense, but it would probably make the theory more adequate.

Are Any Informal Fallacies Committed? Without a fuller exposition of the arguments, pro and con, it may be difficult to determine if there are actually any informal fallacies. However, we are very close to some in typical discussions of this subject. For example, the motives of those who claim to have had an NDE are often questioned by skeptical scientists who say that perhaps these people are just hungry for publicity. If there were no other evidence involved, this would be a reasonable criticism. But since there is more evidence, questioning near-death experiencers' motives alone looks like an *ad hominem* fallacy. Also, do you see any possible question-begging arguments in what we have discussed so far?

An Example of Philosophical
Analysis: Equality of Opportunity

We are often told that equality of opportunity is and ought to be a goal of democracy. A number of writers, however, have questioned the apparent democratic character of this principle. As one states:

> The demand for equality of opportunity may, indeed, wear on the surface of it certain revolutionary aspects; but it is in reality . . . a symptom of . . . unintended conservatism. . . . If the ideal demand of pure democracy were realized, and the social conditions of all men made equal by force of law, there would be no such thing as opportunity, equal or unequal, for anybody. . . . The desire for the right to rise . . . is a desire that everybody . . . shall have an opportunity of achieving by his own talents, if he can, some position or condition which is not equal, but which is, on the contrary, superior to any position or condition which is achievable by the talents of all.[9]

Here we have a type of claim found frequently in philosophical discussion: *What seems to be one type of thing is in reality another sort of thing.* In this case, what is usually classified as a fundamental principle of democracy, equality of opportunity, seems instead to be rather undemocratic. What reasons are given for this shift in

---

[9]W. H. Mallock, *The Limits of Pure Democracy* (London: Chapman and Hall, 1918), p. 280. Mallock is a nineteenth-century British essayist and social critic, widely considered to be one of the most acute critics of democracy and the liberal point of view.

classification—for possibly modifying or reforming our concept of democracy? One is that, at bottom, all of us desire an opportunity to be superior to our fellows. We want an equal start in life so that we can end up as unequals. And there exists an incompatibility between the ideals of democracy and inequality. This much seems implied by the passage.

Claims about what "we all really want"—in this case eventual inequality—should usually be viewed with caution. Is this claim falsifiable, and if so, is there supporting evidence elsewhere? But let us grant that the claim is essentially correct. If it is correct, is it incompatible with our existing beliefs? Does it require that we modify our concept of democracy? Perhaps not.

Consider the following counterargument to the claim that "inequality" and "democracy" are incompatible. We are born with unequal abilities, and certainly we want those of superior ability to be in positions of social, economic, and political leadership, don't we? To attain this end, we should work for equality of opportunity so that the most able among us are in the best position to rise to the top. Viewed in this perspective, equality of opportunity seems perfectly compatible with a feature of democracy, namely, that few of us wish to be ruled by incompetents.

But let's take a second look at our counterargument. Doesn't it contain some questionable assumptions? For example, it seems to assume that most people who rise in the system do so by ability rather than by luck. Does it also assume that we cannot test early on in life who the most able among us will be? If we could determine who are the most able, would not efficiency and fairness require that we promote their abilities with special (unequal) opportunities? In other words is "Equal opportunity for unequal ability" any more self-evident than "Unequal opportunity for unequal ability"?

The author advances a second reason for his claim, one based on an appeal to self-defeating consequences. Ideally, if complete equality of opportunity were realized, the concept of opportunity itself would collapse. All bosses and no workers means that in reality there are no bosses either.

Perhaps we could admit this argument but question its relevance. That is, equality of opportunity is an *ideal*, which in fact may never be reached but toward which we can strive in order to overcome the obvious injustices of inequality of opportunity. If overcoming injustice is a goal of democracy, then certainly there should be room for equal opportunity within the umbrella of democracy.

Still, the idea of Jones insisting that Smith not be given a head start in life just so that he, Jones, can maximize his chances for "rising to the top" strikes us as inconsistent with the spirit of democracy. Is there no way we can reconcile the conflicting points of view involved here? One possibility is this. The problems generated by the equal-opportunity principle are not defects in democracy per se but, rather, are traceable to weaknesses of human nature. Narrowly interpreted, the equality-of-opportunity principle requires merely that we equalize opportunities to satisfy our greed. Broadly interpreted, it helps to ensure that we realize our potential as human beings, including the capacities for love, honesty, and creativity. Perhaps in the end any evaluation of democracy will have to be gauged in the light of democracy's underlying theory of human nature.

VI
Reading Philosophy[1]

Going hand in hand with doing philosophy is the art of reading philosophy. What you read in philosophy naturally provides much of the material with which you can become critically involved. Our survey in Chapters IV and V was mainly concerned with the critical skills of doing philosophy. The present chapter rounds out that survey and gives you some tips on reading philosophy. Our discussion will be divided into four sections: kinds of philosophical writings, preparing to read philosophy, reading for understanding, and reading critically.

Kinds of Philosophical Writings

What counts as a philosophical work depends of course on what counts as philosophy. As you learned in Chapter I, what counts as philosophy is itself a complex question for which there are no absolutely fixed answers. Similarly, there are no hard and fast rules for telling whether a book is or is not a work of philosophy. Philosophy books can be found outside the philosophy sections of libraries, and philosophical arguments can be found outside philosophy books. That a book does not have "philosophy" in its title is no reason to suppose that you will not find interesting philosophical ideas in its pages.

Philosophy books can be divided into two groups, primary and secondary. (This grouping does not take into account reference works, such as philosophical dictionaries and guides to the literature, which

---

[1]This chapter was co-authored by my colleague, Professor Grant Luckhardt.

we shall consider in the next chapter.) The way you read philosophy will depend partly on the type of work you are reading.

Primary Works In primary philosophical works the author presents original arguments and views on a particular topic. For this reason, they may also be referred to as "original" works of philosophy. A primary work may begin with the author's own idea or with someone else's, but its purpose is to arrive at some truth about that idea. Who originally had the idea, or what was thought about it any any point in history, is only of incidental importance in a primary work.

Primary works of philosophy come in three forms: books, articles, and anthologies. Thomas Hobbes's *Leviathan* and Henri Bergson's (1859–1941) *Creative Evolution* are examples of primary *books*. Both authors refer to others' works, either directly or indirectly, but "who said what" is of secondary importance for them. They are primarily concerned with setting forth and adducing reasons for original visions of humanity and the world.

Primary *articles* appear chiefly in philosophical journals, but you can also find philosophically interesting articles in historical, political, literary, and even scientific journals. Most philosophical journals are published four times a year and consist of articles written by teachers of philosophy. (There are also a few journals devoted exclusively to articles by philosophy students.) Journals serve as a forum for philosophical debate, where philosophers can present their ideas for critical examination and comment. Journal articles have the advantage of being shorter than books, letting you get right to the heart of an issue. But they are also more compressed, so that a page of a typical article may take you longer to read and absorb than a page of a typical philosophy book.

Looking beyond primary books and journal articles, you will find primary works in *anthologies*. Anthologies may contain selections from previously published books or journals and may sometimes contain special pieces written just for a particular anthology. They may be devoted to selections from the complete works of a philosopher (for example, devoted to basic writings of Aristotle), from different authors on a given area (for example, readings in moral philosophy), or, finally, from different authors on a variety of topics (for example, introductory readings in philosophy).

Secondary Works Secondary works of philosophy, sometimes called "commentaries," serve as guides to the study of primary works. They may be expositions of philosophers' views, such as you find in a history of philosophy text, and may include relevant questions of historical detail, such as whether Hume ever read Berkeley or whether Plato visited Syracuse on a certain date. Or they may be concerned with matters of interpretation, for example, what Nietzsche means by the 'superman'. Finally, they may be concerned with answering or criticizing what another philosopher or critic has said and may bear such titles as "An Inconsistency in Bergson's Concept of Intuition" or "A Defense of Plato's View That to Harm One's Enemies Is Wrong."

On secondary works a special word of warning is necessary. You should postpone reading secondary interpretations and expositions until you have read the original works. Follow the natural order of things: Read the original first, and only then turn to its interpreters. You are unlikely to learn much about what philosophers have said until you read what they did in fact say. The likelihood is that if you read the commentary first, you will then have to work all the harder when you turn to the original, for then you will be reading the original through someone else's eyes. There are few shortcuts to learning philosophy, but many long ways around. Relying heavily on secondary sources is not a true shortcut to understanding.

There is a special type of secondary work that may legitimately be excepted from the preceding advice. This is the type of work that summarizes particular problems, criticisms, or general viewpoints in philosophy without necessarily claiming to represent the views of any given philosopher. For example, you may read a chapter of a book that summarizes the main themes of a theory called soft determinism. Or you may read an article that presents an overview of different types of existentialism. This type of secondary work can be very helpful if read before or along with your reading of an original work. Many introductory philosophy courses use these summaries together with primary readings. They offer perspective on the general framework within which a given philosopher is working, as well as clues to the types of ideas to look out for. These summaries, of course, like other secondary sources, should be read as a supplement to, not as a substitute for, the original works.

This brings us to our final point. There are many ways to avoid reading original selections of philosophy, if you really wish to. But there are two reasons why it is not in your best interests to do this. First, there is a tremendous sense of personal satisfaction and fulfillment to be had by engaging philosophers directly in their written works. You are forced to turn in upon yourself and to explore attitudes and abilities you may never before have suspected. In this sense, reading original philosophy is (or can be) an exercise in self-realization. Second, by taking the direct route to the philosophers themselves, you will, as a rule, gain a depth and lastingness of knowledge that surpass the superficial understanding reached by way of the shortcuts. Taking shortcuts—for example, turning to an outline of philosophers' principal views—often reduces to a process of memorizing facts that you may or may not understand and may quickly forget. Direct, critical examination of the philosophers themselves is a process that tends to become internalized, that becomes a part of you. And there is no need to emphasize that the direct approach pays handsome rewards when it comes to getting the most out of your philosophy course.

Preparing to Read Philosophy

Reading philosophy can be one of the most challenging and rewarding experiences of your college life. But there are a few obstacles along the way for which you should be prepared. The ideas that philosophers propose and examine can be unusual enough, but the situation is often complicated by the way they express their thoughts. What has come down to us ranges widely from collections of notes prepared by students, to private meditations, to arguments in the style of geometrical proofs, to dialogues, to straightforward prose. You may find not only difficult words but also complicated sentences, sometimes written in the style of another age. Philosophers often take a great deal for granted in their readers as regards both intellectual background and the ability to read well. Usually they expect their readers to be fellow philosophers or intellectuals. The feeling that philosophical writings ought to be instantly understandable may persist because we like to think of ourselves as amateur philosophers. But even amateur philosophizing takes work and practice. And doing this will inevitably involve you in reading works of philosophy, many of which were written in a way to which you may not be accustomed. The following are a few points to keep in mind as you get started.

First, when you sit down to read, give yourself enough time to get into the material—at least an hour, preferably more. As should be clear by now, philosophy involves much more than just soaking up words; you need to go beyond the words to penetrate the ideas themselves. The "twenty-minute scan" approach to a chapter in a history or sociology text, say, may work for those areas sometimes. In philosophy it is worthless. Better not to read at all than to read too hastily in philosophy. Moreover, because reading philosophy requires much concentration, you should choose a time when other matters are not weighing heavily on your mind—to the extent this is possible in college life.

Second, reading philosophy is easier when you keep the momentum going rather than using a stop-and-go approach. In practical terms, this means reading a little philosophy well each day rather than cramming a lot in whenever you can. Of course, keeping the momentum going is good for any subject. However, it is more important to do so in philosophy because of its unusual and sometimes more difficult nature. If you let too much time pass between readings, you will feel that you are always starting over again.

Third, keep a good dictionary handy, as well as a glossary or two of philosophical terms. The dictionary will not help much with technical philosophical terms, but it will be very important in clarifying other unfamiliar terms that may be sprinkled throughout a philosophical piece—terms like 'intrinsic', 'omniscient' or 'ineffable'. For special philosophical terms in the piece you are reading, a glossary should be of some help. But glossaries cannot possibly cover all the terms you will come across, nor do they cover all of the terms' varied meanings.

Finally, as much as possible, keep your personality removed from the material you are reading. As you know by now, in philosophy personal likes and dislikes take a back seat to giving and examining reasons. You are not entering a private debate to be won or lost; you are looking for the most rationally defensible view. If you happen to have any particular attitudes about the subject you are reading, you had best bring them to the surface and reflect on them for a few minutes. The purpose of doing this is not to establish a standard against which to test the reading, to decide, for example, "I'm religiously oriented, so what this philosopher says will be judged accordingly." Rather, the purpose is to help neutralize any biases or inclinations that might unconsciously color your reading, either in favor of or against the author.

Reading for Understanding

The cardinal rule in reading philosophy is to read each work or selection at least twice. Each of these readings should be directed at a different goal. The first should be directed at understanding, the second at criticism. We shall discuss the goal of understanding in this section and the goal of criticism in the next. Our discussion will be geared to primary sources, but much of it will also be applicable to secondary sources.

Reading for understanding begins with an open mind. Since you are attempting in this reading simply to grasp meaning, you should give the author every chance to make that meaning clear to you. There are four ways to reach this goal: (1) develop a preliminary understanding; (2) employ the principle of charity; (3) read actively; and (4) relate passages to relevant ideas. We shall discuss each of these methods in turn.

Develop a Preliminary Understanding Your first task in developing a preliminary understanding is to get a grip on the work or selection as a whole. What is its general perspective? You must see not only the trees but also the forest, and seeing the forest now will help you to see the trees later. Very often the author will have given clues to help you. Such clues may include introductions and tables of contents in books and introductory paragraphs or sections in articles—even the titles of the works themselves. You should read with particular care the introductions, where authors may explain, for example, their point of view or the scope of their work.

Anthologies are a special case since their introductions are written by editors, not the authors themselves. You should not necessarily regard the editor's introduction as stating absolutely what each of the pieces involves, for it is possible for an editor (or anyone) to miss, or misrepresent, one or more of the key ideas in someone else's work. Even the title the editor selects for the piece can have certain connotations that the author might wish to have avoided. Editors can, of course, be very helpful in introducing you to a piece. The advice here is merely that you proceed with caution.

As a second preliminary step, ask yourself how you might argue for the author's thesis. Suppose the author claims that God does not exist. What arguments can you imagine for anyone's claiming this? Have you learned of some arguments from other sources? If so, how might they be used to defend the author's thesis? Taking such a sympathetic stance may be difficult, even impossible when you don't know anything at all about the subject. It may even be distasteful to you and perceived as "dangerous" in some circles. Yet stepping into the author's shoes is worthwhile for two reasons. First, it will help open your mind so that you can better understand the author's claims. Second, it will help you appreciate the author's work when you have understood it. There is no easier way to misunderstand someone than to begin by thinking, "I know what the author's going to say, and I'm certain it can't be true—no matter what reasons the author gives." Your concern in the first reading is with understanding, not with truth.

"Still," you may say, "there are times when I simply cannot deny what I feel about a certain philosophical thesis, no matter what the reasons are." Very well. It is not suggested that you pretend to be somebody you are not. In those cases where you feel very strongly, put that feeling to work; let it motivate you to understand as clearly as possible the author's ideas. Suppose that you have had an abortion and are now reading a piece that is generally antiabortion. Chances are, you will want to refute this thesis and the arguments supporting it. To do this fairly, you will need to understand exactly what it is you are attempting to refute. And so you should want to understand the ideas all the more clearly. Feelings and attitudes may motivate us to be logical and clear-headed, but in philosophy they should not be used as a substitute for either.

A third preliminary in understanding an author consists in getting tips about the author from your instructor. Most philosophers have distinctive styles and strategies in making their points. Knowing about these approaches in advance will help you when you plunge into your reading. For example, the central character in most of Plato's dialogues is his teacher, Socrates, into whose mouth he puts most of his positive philosophical ideas. It is easy to misread Socrates if you do not know about his frequent use of irony—saying one thing and meaning the opposite. For instance, in one dialogue Plato has Socrates heap praise upon one character's ability to make lots of money and his belief that making money is the most important part of life. However, the point of giving such praise is to express the view that moneymaking is one of the least important pursuits in life. Knowing about Plato's use of irony in advance would help you in reading his dialogues.

All of this is well and good, you may say, but in general terms exactly what should we be looking for in developing a preliminary understanding? The answer is threefold. (1) You should have a general idea about the *problem* (or problems) and *subject matter* the author is dealing with and whether they are the same thing. For instance, the problem may be one of justice; the subject matter, fairness. Are they the same thing? (2) You should have some idea about the *conclusions* that will be defended— for instance, that justice and fairness overlap but are not identical. What is the author trying to prove or defend? (3) You should have some idea about *how* the author intends to proceed. Does the author argue by describing cases that seem to involve fairness but not justice? What are his or her reasons? Of course, these three areas may often be complicated, and the answers to your questions far from clear-cut. But you should strive to develop some understanding in each of these areas nonetheless.

Employ the Principle of Charity Having developed some preliminary understanding, you should use what is called the principle of charity as you read a work. Observing this principle, you should at first construe the text in the most favorable reading. When the text admits of different interpretations, or seems to make little sense in places, or appears contradictory in others, then you should read it in a way that helps make sense and avoids inconsistencies—in short, you should give it the interpretation that would make the author most correct. The principle of charity requires that when you encounter such difficulties in a text, you should assume at first—though you need not in the end—that the fault lies with you and that it is you who have failed to understand something.

When confronted with passages that seem to make little sense, it is all too easy to conclude that the author is wrong, or foolish, or whatever. Fairness and prudence, however, require that you hold off your critical reading until later. Since you primarily want to understand at this point, you should give the author every benefit of the doubt. Of course, if there are glaring problems, such as a flat contradiction or invalid inference, you should make a note of it so that you can return to consider it later. If you give the author the benefit of the doubt now, your criticisms later will be all the stronger, being based on the best possible interpretation of what he says now.

For some practice, let's examine a passage from the British philosopher George Berkeley (1685–1753) and a mistaken criticism that it generated.

> It is indeed an opinion strangely prevailing amongst men
> that houses, mountains, rivers, and, in a word, all sensible
> objects have an existence, natural or real, distinct from
> their being perceived by the understanding. . . . *[Yet]*
> what are the forementioned objects but the things we perceive by sense? And what do we perceive besides our own

ideas or sensations? And is it not plainly repugnant that any one of these, or any combination of them, should exist unperceived?[2]

This passage from Berkeley, as well as his whole defense of subjective idealism, is remarkable; it states in effect that so-called material things cannot exist unless they are perceived. Now, it is very easy to misinterpret Berkeley, to level criticism too hastily. Picking up on such claims as "We only perceive our own ideas," the British writer Samuel Johnson is reputed to have set aside his copy of Berkeley, walked outside, kicked a stone, and declared, "Thus, I refute Berkeley." Did he? Nothing Berkeley says in this passage or elsewhere suggests that stones, chairs, food, houses, mountains are not compact, hard, or solid. Did Johnson think that Berkeley held that material objects are nothing more than ghostlike entities, that he should be able to walk through walls? If so, he did not give Berkeley the benefit of the doubt and try to make sense of his remarks in the light of his whole work. If Johnson had been more charitable, so to speak, he would never have produced such a misinformed "refutation" of Berkeley.

Read Actively   Reading philosophy actively means that you are continuously involved in understanding or examining the material at hand. You are not a passive observer, hoping the words will somehow speak for themselves. Reading philosophy is definitely not like reading a newspaper or a history textbook. We shall consider three ways of reading philosophy actively for understanding.

First, you should make every effort to keep a set of reading notes, or journal, as you read, in whatever format is most convenient for you. Such notes will preserve a record of your understanding, questions, critical remarks, and possible misunderstandings. They will be potentially helpful for class discussion, term papers, and tests, and well as for your own learning experience. Your notes should begin with a general statement on what the work is all about. This will be based upon the preliminary clues already discussed. You should leave some room on the page for possible revisions as you proceed, for your interpretation may change considerably as your understanding deepens. Each major paragraph and section of the work should be represented in your notes, sometimes with a sentence or two and sometimes with a longer exposition. The first and last sentences of the paragraphs and sections will often contain the key points.

Now, there is an important qualification in this procedure. If it is to be successful, you must enter all the key ideas in your own words, with the exception of exact definitions stated by the author. It is a sure

[2]George Berkeley, *A Treatise Concerning the Principles of Human Knowledge* (New York: Liberal Arts Press, 1957), p. 24.

sign that you have not understood the author very well if the only way you can express ideas is in the author's words. To understand something is to be able to relate it to something else, to other words, facts, ideas, actions. If you cannot relate a passage to anything—that is, if you cannot state the underlying meaning in your own words—then you haven't understood very well. This is the acid test in philosophy, whether you are studying for a test, writing a paper, or reading a work. Of course, you are not necessarily expected to write out the author's point as well or as elegantly as the author. But this is not important now. What is important is that you begin to state ideas in your own words.

Obviously, not everything the author says will be of equal importance. There may actually be quite a bit of sidetracking off to this or that little detail. In general, however, you should be on the lookout for six related items for your journal:

1. Definitions: "By 'morally right' I mean . . ."
2. Distinctions: "In order to see why philosopher X is mistaken, we should keep in mind the difference between actions done by oneself and actions done for oneself."
3. Conclusions or main themes: "If my arguments are sound, it would appear that religion is not necessary to give meaning to life."
4. Arguments: "If God is dead, and morality is based on religion, then anything is permitted." (*Not a sound argument*)
5. Overall significance, from the author's perspective: "I may not have shown that materialism is true, but I have at least given reasons for supposing that dualism is false."
6. Kinds of claims made: "Most people in the world have some religious belief" (*empirical*), "If you don't believe in God you can't be religious" (*a priori*, implying a definition), "If you make a promise, then you ought to keep it." (*normative*)

Of course, your journal will contain other kinds of information, too; but if you read actively and *purposively*, looking for definitions, arguments, and so forth, then your understanding will be increased, and your notebook will be more than just disconnected sentences. For practice, let's read through the following passage from the French existentialist Jean-Paul Sartre (1905–1980):

Man is nothing else but what he makes of himself. Such is the first principle of existentialism. . . . But what do we mean by this, if not that man has a greater dignity than a stone or table? For we mean that man first exists, that is, that man first of all is the being who hurls himself toward a future and who is conscious of imagining himself as being in the future. Man is at the start a plan which is aware of itself, rather than a patch of moss, a piece of garbage, or a cauliflower.[3]

Like most philosophical passages, this one will come more clearly into focus as you read further. Yet even in the space of a few short sentences, Sartre has covered quite a bit of ground. Your reading notes might include the following: "First principle of existentialism: Man is the being who makes himself. Man differs from other objects in that he (1) has greater dignity, (2) conceives of his future, and (3) is aware of himself. Sartre emphasizes self-determination, but what about environmental conditioning?" Of course, your own notes might include more or fewer comments. Note, however, the quality of this journal entry. It has not only captured the main points in the paragraph but it has also ordered and posed them in a creative way that shows that the reader has worked at understanding rather than merely repeated what Sartre said. In addition, in the last sentence of the entry, a critical question is raised that may require attention at a later time.

Should you not have the time to keep a notebook or set of reading notes, you may find it helpful to use a second, shorter method. This is the method of stating out loud the main points of key paragraphs, sections, and chapters. It is absolutely necessary that you say, rather than merely think, what the point is. Speak to a friend, a wall or mirror, anything, but say it aloud. Thinking it silently to yourself usually just does not work well unless you are already an advanced student of philosophy. Keeping it to yourself allows too much fudging with half-baked ideas and intuitions, often backed up with some often misplaced reassurance like "Oh well, I know what I mean." When you hear what you are thinking, it will appear quite different to you and force you to be a little more honest with yourself. Try it and see!

Finally, there is the old standby method, that of underlining or "highlighting" passages and making marginal notes. It takes less time but tends also to be less helpful than the other approaches. This is because underlining in particular has a way of simply drawing one's attention to a passage without requiring much intellectual involvement. Of course, with this method, as with the others, you will be looking for the key factors: definitions, arguments, overall significance. Keep in mind that too much underlining serves no purpose; it won't magically transform those words into clear understanding. In particular, too much underlining is self-defeating; it blurs the contrast between what is important and what is secondary. And keeping that contrast in reasonably sharp focus will greatly aid the process of reading for understanding.

[3]Jean-Paul Sartre, *Existentialism and Human Emotions* (New York: Philosophical Library, 1957), p. 15.

Relate Passages to Relevant Ideas   A final way of reading for understanding is to relate the passage either to other philosophers' ideas or to logically connected thoughts in the work itself. This approach is implied by the other approaches we have considered. Using it effectively, however, assumes that you are already fairly well along in your study of a given philosopher or issues. So you would never use this strategy at the very beginning of your study of a whole new area of philosophy, and you would always use it in addition to some other approaches. We shall now consider three rules of thumb.

The first way to relate a passage to other ideas is to attach a label to it, perhaps one of the isms you have already learned about. Of course, labels are only general approximations, but they do help to stay in the ball park. Suppose that you are reading about the psychologist B. F. Skinner's denial of human freedom. Well, in what sense is he denying freedom—that advocated by a **soft determinist** or that denied by a **hard determinist**? Which is Skinner? Perhaps he doesn't fit neatly in either category. So you resolve to read further. Even if the label you eventually decide on doesn't exactly fit, you are a little closer to understanding what Skinner is up to.

The second way to relate a passage to other ideas is the familiar one of comparing and contrasting it, usually with the ideas of other philosophers. Sometimes the ideas of a familiar writer outside philosophy are also good points of reference. You ask how a certain idea is similar to, or different from, a related idea. This approach is closely related to the method of labeling. For example, how does Aristotle's conception of 'substance' differ from Plato's? Or suppose you are reading John Stuart Mill's defense of what the consequences of a morally right act ought to be. From your reading or from lectures by your instructor, you may know that Mill took over the utilitarian movement started by Jeremy Bentham. How, then, does Mill appear to be changing Bentham's conception of "the greatest amount of pleasure for the greatest number of persons"? Comparing and contrasting are always good strategies to use in improving your understanding of a philosopher's work.

The third way to relate a passage is to try to place it in some type of logical perspective within the work you are reading. Providing a logical perspective involves placing an idea in a continuum. At one end of the continuum will be those ideas or arguments that seem to suggest or imply the idea in question. At the other end will be those considerations that seem to follow from or be implied by the idea in question. You need not be overly concerned with strict logic here. The more general question you will ask about the passage is this: "Within the text I'm now reading, where does this idea seem to be coming from, and where does it seem to be leading, if anywhere?"

How would you apply this strategy? Imagine, for example, that you are reading a passage by the philosopher David Hume (1711–1776) and read of his rejection of the personal self. You read that whenever he "looks" for his inner self (soul), he cannot find it and concludes that it must therefore not exist. Taken by itself, this seems a strange claim. Hume cannot find himself, his "I." Who is doing the looking? By placing the statement in context, it is easier to see what he is up to. For his claim follows from his general operating assumption that to every idea—in this case the idea of the self as a substantial thing—there must correspond an immediate impression in direct experience. And it leads to the claim that the self is not a "thing" in its own right but a bundle of memories and experiences stretched out over time. So Hume is not denying that he exists, only denying that he exists as a certain type of thing, a soul. This still may not appear very plausible, but it does make more sense within its context or logical perspective.

We should emphasize that none of the preceding rules of thumb can be mechanically or indiscriminately applied to a philosophical work with the expectation of immediate results. Each sentence and paragraph is not necessarily going to make sense right away—or even be very important. Reading a philosophy work for understanding is more like piecing together a puzzle than being presented with a completed painting.

Reading Critically

After you have completed your first reading or understood the selection as best you can (which may actually require several readings), you should read it again with a critical eye. To read critically is not to proceed sword in hand, ready to attack every statement that confronts you. Rather, it is to exercise your judgment in determining both what is important and whether the important points are correct or plausible. In the end, your judgment may be that the author is essentially right, or partially right and partially wrong, or simply altogether wrong. You do not read critically just to produce refutations.

How does one read critically? The question has already been largely answered in earlier chapters. Reading philosophy critically is doing philosophy. A review of the strategies described there will always be helpful. Here we need only pinpoint the most important questions you should have in mind during a critical reading. Briefly, they are (1) Are the main points clear? (2) Are the main points or conclusions supported with plausible reasons? (3) Are there weaknesses the author may not have considered, such as faulty assumptions? (4) How close does the work come to doing what it sets out to do? (5) Can you support your criticisms of the work with good reasons? To be sure, these are not the only questions you will want to consider. But they are the most important and will get you off to a good start.

Doing philosophy and reading philosophy are different sides of the same coin. There is, however, a "third" side, namely, writing philosophy, in which the results of your reading and doing philosophical work are distilled out in distinct form. It is to that third side that we turn in the next chapter. Once you have understood what reading, writing, and doing philosophy involve, you will have understood the heart of philosophy.

VII
Writing Philosophy[1]

Preparing to write one's first philosophy essay usually raises a number of important questions. Is this like writing a research paper? Does the instructor just want my opinion about a certain issue? How do I get started? Am I supposed to improve on the views of professional philosophers? The purpose of this chapter is to help you understand what is normally expected when you are asked to write a critical philosophy essay. You will also find some practical rules to follow as you write your paper. These rules should help you when you write an examination essay, too.

The Nature of a Critical
Philosophy Essay

The central purpose of a philosophy paper is unlike that of many term papers you may have been assigned in courses other than philosophy; it is usually *critical* rather than *reportive*. Reportive work generally takes two forms: either expressing your personal viewpoint on an assigned topic, such as love, or compiling and organizing the results of laboratory work or of book research on a topic such as the economic causes of social unrest. In both forms one simply presents the facts as one understands them or as someone else does. Your

---

[1]This chapter was originally coauthored by Professor Steven M. Sanders of the Department of Philosophy, Bridgewater State College, Bridgewater, Massachusetts.

philosophy instructor may, of course, assign a purely reportive project. This chapter deals essentially with critical philosophy papers, however.

A critical philosophy essay involves much more than simply presenting your own opinions and the views of relevant philosophers on a take-it-or-leave-it basis. Instead, you question and become intellectually involved with your subject matter, taking little for granted. Specifically, there are five primary rules to follow in writing a critical philosophy essay. Firstly, you must *clarify* key ideas. For instance, are the philosophically troublesome terms defined? Are the theories in question exemplified and presented in straightforward language? Secondly, you must test the soundness of the arguments for or against the theories in question. Are the inferences valid? Are the premises true? Thirdly, you must evaluate the theories, using some of the methods discussed in Chapter IV of this book. Are the assumptions correct? Are the consequences plausible? Fourthly, and most important, you must support what you assert with reasons. Are your claims backed up with arguments? Do they follow from other claims already established? Finally, it is important to defend your position against the best possible arguments that might be raised in opposition to it. Try to anticipate potential misinterpretations and criticisms and decide how you would attempt to deal with them. This will assist you in recognizing opposing points of view as well as potential weaknesses in your own arguments and position. To summarize: Whereas in a reportive paper you organize and pass on others' thoughts, in a critical philosophy essay you think for yourself, though not in a vacuum.

The topic of rational *support* is especially important. Many students tend to rely on certain illegitimate methods to support a position. Here we note five such methods. In particular, you should not support your case merely by

1. Labeling the case your own
2. Asserting the case's superiority over the competition
3. Using *ad hominem* arguments, that is, attacking a person's character or circumstances, rather than that person's arguments
4. Citing an authority, whether philosophical or scientific
5. Exemplifying the case or defining its key terms

The defects of the first three methods are for the most part self-evident. The other two methods, insofar as they are, in themselves, the more legitimate, scholarly approaches, can also be the more deceptive. Consider the fourth method. Remember that citing a philosophical authority carries little weight if you do not also adduce arguments, for even the greatest philosophers' views can be questioned. Citing a scientific authority, meanwhile, is usually sufficient to attest to the truth of certain empirical facts, but as you will recall from Chapter I, those facts do not entail the truth of any particular philosophical theory. Turning to the fifth method, remember that by illustrating your position and defining the key terms, you are only helping your readers to understand what you are arguing for, not why they should accept it. We considered the correct use of examples and definitions in Chapter IV.

The following passage, which contains no arguments (no conclusions derived from premises), illustrates some of the incorrect methods of supporting a position. The numbers in parentheses indicate the relevant defect.

> Let me support the view known as **ethical relativism**. The truth of ethical relativism is shown by the fact that two persons might disagree over the moral rightness of a certain act and, if they are from different cultures or backgrounds, both may be correct (5). Now anyone who denies this is authoritarian (3). Who am I to condemn the Eskimos for leaving their aged relatives on the ice to die? Moreover, anthropologists have been telling us for a long time that ethical relativism is true (4). Finally, the only alternative to ethical relativism is **ethical absolutism**, and we know absolutism is false (2).

Many students worry about producing a critical philosophy essay because they fear that their labors will be evaluated according to their instructor's personal beliefs. Let us emphasize, however, that your essay will be analyzed on the basis of objective criteria. For example, have you written clearly? Is your case supported with arguments? Have you fairly and accurately presented others' views? Is your essay well organized? Have you attempted to think for yourself instead of just parroting the views of other philosophers? Your essay will not be evaluated on the basis of your personal convictions or those of your instructor. Whether or not your instructor agrees with the general position you advance is largely irrelevant. In fact, instructors prefer that you rationally support a theory that they think is false rather than merely present a view that they believe is true.

Organizing Your Essay

Putting together a coherent, well-organized philosophy essay is not a simple and clear-cut task. This section will discuss five organizational strategies that may help you organize your essay. The strategies are these: (1) formulating the problem; (2) deciding on a format; (3) incorporating other philosophers' views; (4) presenting a good introduction; and (5) achieving coherence.

Formulating the Problem Critical philosophy essays involve responses to philosophical problems. If it has not been done already, your first task should be to translate the general problem or topic about which you are writing into a specific *question* or *statement*. Suppose, for example, that you are asked to write a critical essay on the problem of evil. You should first ask yourself exactly what questions this problem involves. In the case of the problem of evil, a relevant question would be, "How can God's perfect nature, particularly His moral character, be reconciled with the existence of evil in the world?" Then again, you may wish to focus critical attention on a certain controversial response to that question. If so, this response must be translated into a specific statement—for example, "Human beings, not God, are responsible for evil through the depraved exercise of their free will"—which may then be either attacked or defended. Performing such preliminary "translations" will give you a focal point around which to organize your essay and will help prevent your drifting from the issue during the course of your analysis.

Once you have formulated the specific question or statement with which you will be dealing, you should then clarify the key terms. A lack of clarity in the initial formulation of the problem can affect the organization and direction of your essay. To continue with our original example, consider the term 'evil'. So long as we restrict ourselves to a certain kind of evil, namely, moral evil, such as lying and murder, it is easier to suppose that human beings are responsible for introducing evil in what was originally a perfect world. But even if we accept this response at face value and we do not question the assumption of free will, the restriction to moral evil only partially resolves the problem. Why? Because it does not account for natural evil such as disease. Surely human beings are not responsible for disease. Wouldn't God remain responsible for natural evil? Answers to questions involving one kind of evil do not automatically transfer to questions involving another kind. Distinguishing between the kinds of evil at the beginning of your analysis would probably require you to limit your investigation to one variety or else to adopt a different strategy that will enable you to reconcile both types of evil with God's moral perfection. Initial clarity greatly improves organizational strategy. Clarity is discussed in more detail in the next section.

Having clarified the key terms, you should next think through the assumptions of the question you are attempting to answer. How do they influence the kinds of answers that might be given? For example, the question "Why did God create the world with so much evil?" tends to lock one into a fairly narrow range of answers, all involving God's motives. A natural response that uncritically takes the question at face value is, "Because God wanted a testing ground for distinguishing between the worthy and the not so worthy." A critical look at the assumptions of the question, however, might easily have led you either to reformulate it or to raise a different issue altogether. The question "Why did God create the world with so much evil?" already presupposes affirmative answers to the questions "Does God exist?" "Did

God create the world?" "Is God responsible for evil?" and even "Does evil exist?" If good reasons can be found for answering any of these questions in the negative—for example, reasons for concluding that God is not responsible for evil—then the original question about why He created a world with evil collapses. You will find it helpful, then, to consider the assumptions implied in your initial formulation of the problem before writing your essay. And you may or may not find it necessary to reformulate the problem.

Deciding on a Format Closely related to formulating the problem is deciding on an appropriate format for developing your ideas. Probably the most commonly adopted formats are these: (1) comparing and contrasting two or more theories—for example, two attempted resolutions of the problem of evil—in order to determine the most adequate among them; (2) criticizing a single theory or argument; (3) defending another philosopher's view against mistaken criticism; and (4) supporting and defending an original theory of your own.

You must decide which of these (or other) formats best suits your interests and abilities. Remember, however, that philosophy is a cumulative activity wherein one comes closer to the truth by avoiding the mistakes of other philosophers. So if you do not know where to begin, the most fruitful strategy for your first essay will probably be to criticize views that seem to you mistaken. Why? Because you already have at your disposal those critical techniques discussed earlier. By asking yourself, "Does this argument appear sound?" and "Are the consequences of this view plausible?" you may take an important first step in thinking for yourself.[2] Also, if you avoid the criticism applicable to implausible views, the lines along which your own thesis must be developed will emerge naturally.

Incorporating Other Philosophers' Views In organizing your paper, you may find yourself asking: "How am I supposed to improve on the theories of philosophers who have spent their lives thinking about these issues? Even where I think one philosopher is wrong, it seems that all I can do is quote another philosopher to support my contention. I have thought about the issue and in my opinion philosopher X's arguments are correct, so here they are." Beginning students in philosophy are not expected to revolutionize philosophy. Your instructor is interested primarily in getting you to begin thinking for yourself. But provided that you do not repeat others'

---

[2]You will probably want to consider other critical questions, too. For example: "Do the arguments show something other than what they are intended to show?" "Has the writer properly interpreted the problem?" "Are central claims mutually consistent?" "Has the writer subtly changed the meaning of key terms?" "Is the theory sufficiently developed and exemplified?"

views unquestioningly, and provided that you give credit where it is due—especially when paraphrasing or using direct quotations—it is natural that you will use the arguments of other philosophers. No writer on philosophical problems works in a vacuum.

Most importantly, the objection to incorporating other philosophers' views involves a false assumption. Exercising one's own problem-solving abilities is not incompatible with bringing in other philosophers' theories and arguments. Incorporating other views is not an all-or-nothing proposition. Often, your paper will blend or synthesize your thinking with the views about which you have read. For example, you may defend another person's theory against unsound criticism with your own arguments. Other possible blends are (1) restating a philosopher's arguments or theory in a clearer, more incisive, way; (2) applying that argument or theory to areas not discussed by its original proponent; (3) admitting the view is mistaken in places but attempting to remedy those deficiencies and thus produce a modified view.

Presenting a Good Introduction Once you have thought through the problem, determined the general conclusions you wish to argue for, and decided on a format for developing your ideas, you should be ready to express the results of your preliminary investigation in a good introduction. A good introduction has several virtues. First, it helps keep your essay on the right track. That is, if you commit yourself to showing that a certain thesis is false, then that is what you must do. The chances are much greater that your essay will lack coherence and direction if you do not spell out your commitments in advance. Second, it gives the reader some assurance that you know what you are about to undertake.

There is no exact format for good introductions. They should, however, clearly set out the following: (1) the problem to which you will address yourself; (2) what you intend to show, for example, that a theory should be modified or that one theory is preferable to another; and (3) how you propose to do this, for example, by showing that one theory rests on highly questionable assumptions. Each of the three points is made clear in the sample introduction that follows:

> In his novel about a behaviorally engineered utopia, *Walden II*, B. F. Skinner claims through one of its central characters that if man is free then a science of human behavior is impossible. Since Skinner believes that a science of psychology is possible, he draws the inference that man is not free. While his thesis may be supportable on other grounds, I propose to demonstrate in this paper that Skinner's reasons for denying human freedom are not persuasive. After presenting his view in more detail, I shall argue that his case rests on faulty assumptions concerning the nature of freedom and the purpose of

science. A science of psychology, we shall see, is quite compatible with human freedom.

Achieving Coherence   Many undergraduate papers in philosophy suffer from a lack of coherence and incisiveness—what we may call a "drifting" phenomenon. Your reader becomes puzzled over where you are and what you are doing. Undefined terms appear from nowhere. Arguments appear out of nowhere, with little or no indication of what they are supposed to show. The same point is rehashed five different ways. Examples are inserted randomly. Too much territory is covered in a single sentence or paragraph. Too much writing is devoted to inessential points or perhaps to saying nothing. These are just some of the manifestations of drifting.

Of course, this phenomenon is by no means unique to philosophy papers. It tends to occur more frequently in students' philosophy papers, however, because of the relative novelty of the subject matter and the intellectual discipline required to produce a good philosophy essay. After you have written your first draft, therefore, go through it again, sentence by sentence, paragraph by paragraph, and ask yourself the following questions: What is the relevance of this passage, and does it clearly fit here? Is the passage an essential link in my argument? Is it used to clarify? Does it tell the reader where I am and where I'm going? If it is an argument, is its relevance to what I'm trying to show clear? Does this sentence add anything to the substance of my essay? Does my introduction get the point? Your responses to these questions will probably mean rewriting or deleting some passages. Doing so, however, will help greatly to tighten the organization of your paper.

Achieving Clarity

In the preceding section we considered ways to organize an essay. Sound organization is essential for communicating your ideas effectively in a philosophy essay and in itself contributes greatly to the overall clarity (and persuasiveness) of your essay. Our concern in this section, however, is primarily with the clarity of individual words and sentences. We shall consider the following areas: (1) ensuring that key terms clearly express the ideas they are supposed to convey, (2) using examples properly, and (3) improving your style of writing.

Clearly Expressing Your Ideas   Clear writing presupposes clear understanding; if you do not understand the point you attempt to get across, you can hardly expect your reader to be enlightened, no matter how pleasing your style of expression may be. There is no foolproof procedure for gaining this prerequisite understanding. But rereading your sources, participating in "think sessions" with your friends, conferring with your instructor, and applying some of the critical questions discussed in Chapters IV and V—all these strategies should help. "Think sessions," whether personal or collective, are especially important, for in philosophy it is easy to believe that you clearly understand key ideas because you have memorized words—when in fact you do not. This is why "cramming" for philosophy exams is often ineffective.

Once you know what you wish to say, you will want to consider how you can communicate your ideas most effectively. If you do not express yourself clearly, your reader will usually assume that you do not fully understand your topic. Clarity of expression at the beginning is always preferable to later debates over whether one really understood what one was writing about. Most instructors are unmoved by such pleas from students as "Come on, now, you know what I meant!" The most likely response is, "Well, why didn't you write what you meant?" Following are a few rules of thumb that will help you present a clear statement of your ideas.

Firstly, avoid vagueness, particularly of key terms and sentences. A vague expression is one whose meaning is not clear because it fails to specify exactly to what objects or circumstances it should be applied. Vague ideas are "rough" ideas. For example, a vague idea of 'democracy' is "a political system in which the people have something to say about how they are governed." Although this conception of democracy is not incorrect, it needs considerable refinement. Who, for instance, are "the people"—those educated enough to vote intelligently or sufficiently well-off to pay taxes without going hungry? Are we talking about a majority of people? If so, may they exterminate the minority? How much voice may they have in being governed? Did Hitler's Germany qualify as a democracy because "the people" freely chose Hitler as their leader? Vagueness can be reduced by providing adequate definitions, using examples, restating your point in a different way—in short, by spelling out in detail what you mean.

Secondly, avoid ambiguity. Ambiguity occurs when the reader is unsure which among several possible meanings of an expression is intended, although each meaning may be relatively clear by itself. A common fallacy of ambiguity is to begin an essay using a term to mean one thing and then to switch implicitly to another meaning without informing your reader. For example, a student recently wrote an essay in which he sometimes used the term "mind" in a collective sense to mean "the sum total of one's particular experiences, dispositions, and thoughts" and at other times used it in a substantial sense connoting a thing, "a container or repository of particular thoughts and experiences." Such ambiguous expression greatly reduces clarity.

Thirdly, minimize your use of technical or profound-sounding expressions. When you must use them, clarify them immediately. A few examples of such expressions are 'reality', 'absolute', 'subjective', 'essence', 'inner self', 'cosmic', 'power structure', and 'establishment mentality'. Covering as much territory as they do, they are often unsuitable for precisely formulating and analyzing a problem. Unless you clearly fix their meaning, their elasticity is such that they are open to a variety of connotations, which will both confuse your readers and allow them to read too much into your view. Such expressions lend themselves to vagueness and ambiguity. For these reasons, avoid also such clichés as "Seeing is believing" or "It all depends on your point of view." These reveal your unwillingness to think through what you are writing.

Fourthly, do not rely heavily on metaphors and analogies. For example, time has been metaphorically depicted as a river that passes from out of the future into the past. And the world has been compared to a giant, complex machine. Although metaphors and analogies are often helpful in presenting philosophical ideas, their capacity to enlighten is equaled by their capacity to mislead. The world is not just like a machine. Some have argued that without human interference, nature's balance exhibits an efficient order and continuity unmatched by any machine. Depending on the point you wish to make, you may decide to drop the analogy altogether, considering all the ways in which the world is and is not like a machine. Metaphors and analogies should be used in addition to, never in place of, straightforward argumentation.

Finally, make what you mean and what your words mean harmonize. Choose your words carefully and write exactly what you mean. For example, you may wish to describe a kleptomaniac as one who does not act freely. You may express this by saying that the kleptomaniac steals "automatically." But this expression does not say what you want to say, because there is no incompatibility between acting freely and acting automatically. What you probably mean is that the kleptomaniac acts compulsively, though what your words mean is that the person acts without deliberation, spontaneously. So it is important to keep in mind that the words you use may mean something that you do not intend to convey. To help avoid this situation, ask yourself, "What do I want to say?" and "How can I say it most effectively?"

Precision is most important in philosophy. Avoid careless expression by rereading your written work. To take another example, a student recently wrote: "The materialist believes that the body is a physical entity. There is no separation from the body of the soul at death." Here the instructor would know what the student wants to say (or at least ought to be saying), but the statement is poorly suited to its purpose. For instance, the dualist also believes that the body is a physical entity, but holds that there is in addition a nonphysical aspect, a mind or soul. What the student meant to say was, "The materialist believes that persons are physical entities, nothing more." Furthermore, from the second sentence in the student's passage it seems as though there is a soul that just doesn't happen to leave the body at the time of death. The student should have said more straightforwardly, "There is no soul or mind that survives the death of the body." So once again, express yourself carefully.

Using Examples   In Chapter IV we noted how examples help to clarify meaning. Using examples is particularly important in writing your philosophy essay. Appropriate examples will reduce vagueness and help to keep both you and your reader from getting lost in generalities and abstractions. The following are three points to bear in mind when you use examples.

First, remember that examples are not arguments, but illustrative devices. They do not demonstrate the truth of your case; they help to clarify meaning. For instance, citing Jesus, Socrates, and Gandhi may help to illustrate what you mean by the expression "social revolutionary." But doing so does not prove that these three men were, in fact, social revolutionaries. To prove that, argumentation is required.

Second, it is often helpful to think through the relation between the example you cite and what it is supposed to exemplify. This helps to avoid confusion and increase precision. For instance, your essay may revolve around the concept of a supreme being. As particular examples, you cite God, Allah, and Brahman. But these are examples of very different types of supreme beings. In fact, the impersonal Brahman differs so radically from the colorful creator Allah that Brahman probably should not be classified as a supreme being at all. So if your discussion refers only to the concept of a creator-God to which we ascribe certain humanlike qualities, citing Brahman would probably confuse your reader, not clarify your case.

Finally, it is important that your examples be specific enough to carry the weight of illustration. For instance, if you attempt to show what it would be like to act always according to the golden rule, you must give enough detail to tell your reader what acting according to such a rule would actually come to. To be more specific, would judges have to release criminals on the grounds that they, the judges, would not want to be sent to prison themselves? Or is this a misapplication of the golden rule? Tying your case down to particular examples will increase clarity.

Writing Well   In closing, it may be helpful to mention a few matters regarding your style of writing. Entire books have been devoted to the topics of writing style and grammar.[3] The following are a few practical suggestions on clear writing.

Firstly, unless you are a relatively polished writer, keep your sentences short. Doing so will help you to express one idea at a time

---

[3]A helpful, concise text devoted to elementary rules of style and grammar is William Strunk, Jr., and E. B. White, *The Elements of Style*, 3rd ed. (New York: Macmillan, 1979). A widely used text about the mechanics of constructing term papers is Kate Turabian, *A Manual for Writers of Term Papers, Theses, and Dissertations*, 3rd ed. (Chicago: University of Chicago Press, 1967). A delightful work with many helpful tips is Brand Blanshard, *On Philosophical Style* (Bloomington, Ind.: Indiana University Press, 1967).

and thereby increase precision. Similarly, avoid wordiness. For example, consider the poorly executed sentence "What we see out there in the external world is really there"; written simply as "We see the world as it is," it still expresses the same point.

Secondly, use transitional devices, such as "Let us now turn to our first argument" and "Following my presentation of theory X, I shall offer two criticisms of it." Using devices that tell your reader where you've been and where you expect to go will help keep both of you on track as you guide the reader naturally through the sections of your paper to the conclusion. Also, in longer essays it can be helpful to stop occasionally to summarize in a brief paragraph or two the substance of your argument up to that point.

Thirdly, do not pad your essay with useless additions, such as too many examples for a single point, apologies for not having shown more than you did, restatements of the obvious, and extended quotations. Quotations should be included only when there is a reason for giving someone's exact words—for example, when a question of interpretation is at issue. Padding diverts your reader's interest from the important points you wish to make.

Fourthly, write in the active voice rather than in the passive voice. Although writing in the passive voice is not necessarily less clear, too much passive voice fatigues your reader and is less likely to make a forceful impression. For example, instead of writing, "Theory X was earlier shown by me to be false," write, "I have demonstrated that theory X is false."

Fifthly, don't overwork indefinite terms such as "this," "that," "which," "thing," and "idea"; be specific. Of course, such terms are sound aids to normal exposition. When overused, however, they frequently generate vagueness and confusion, requiring the reader to puzzle out what they refer to. Suppose in examining a theory, you cite two philosophical claims and then state, "I shall now argue that this is false." Here, the antecedent is ambiguous, for it is not clear whether "this" refers to both claims or to one of them or, if it refers to one of them, which one it refers to. As an alternative, you might say, "I shall now argue that the second claim, 'The end always justifies the means', is false."

Finally, consider visiting your school's writing center. This will help with matters of grammar, style, and possibly overall argumentative strategy. It will also allow your instructor to focus more on the substance of your philosophical points.

In conclusion, we have surveyed a few of the points that will help you develop your philosophy essay. You have not been offered a foolproof method or mechanical procedure for writing philosophy clearly and coherently, for no such method exists. Philosophical ability, as manifested in clear and cogent thinking and writing, is one of the arts of life—to be cultivated by anyone who has the willingness to think and the spirit to endeavor.

A Sample Essay

The following is a very brief hypothetical essay. For purposes of illustration, it contains far more mistakes and deficiencies than would normally appear in a single paper. The important point is to understand and avoid the mistakes included. These are enumerated at the end of the draft. Corresponding to each number in the draft is a statement of the relevant mistake. Some of the shortcomings, including those of a stylistic nature, are noted for the first time. A rewritten draft is then presented. Although it is not intended as a piece of professional philosophy and is open to criticism, the new draft is a substantial improvement in both style and content. Some potentially good points made in the first draft are retained, the more questionable ones abandoned. The revised draft represents a reasonable ideal to strive for in your own expression.

Preliminary Draft

Through the ages people have asked what is right and what is wrong (1). Abortion is one of those questions (2). Now it seems to me (3) that abortion is morally right (4), especially since the Supreme Court ruling outlawed antiabortion laws in various states (5). There is lots of evidence to show that this is so. Once some of this evidence is presented, any thinking person (6) should favor abortion. Of course, since this is a philosophical problem and we are all entitled to our own opinions on such matters (7), about all I can do is present my views and hope that the reader will be convinced (8).

I'll begin by noting the influence of religious beliefs upon the question of abortion (9). For example, concern over the soul of an aborted fetus has led (10) to an attitude completely insensitive to the problems of the here and the now. For example, what happens to unwanted children (11)? Does anybody in his right mind think this is good (12)? Besides, I don't think religion should take precedence over a mother's right to control her own body (13).

To prove my point, let's consider the following example in detail (14). Mary Jones decided she did not want any children. Yet unfortunately she got pregnant. When she thought about getting an abortion, however, she felt guilty because society, which is filled with religious beliefs such as fear of God, made her feel guilty (15). So she had the child. But since it was not wanted and was retarded, she took very poor care of it and placed the responsibilities of motherhood on schoolteachers, babysitters, and the like. Eventually he became a burden to society. The fact that she was in part responsible for this outcome in turn made Mary's life miserable all because the original decision was through social pressure taken out of her hands (16).

They say that attitudes about abortion are more liberal these days (17). Certainly, the fact that more and more women are getting abortions these days shows that it's becoming more and more moral (18). But those who are against abortion still do not seem to perceive that their position rests on a contradiction (19). We grant women rights to choose their spouses, careers, and lifestyles, to take care of or mistreat their bodies, and raise children as they see fit. Why should we force on them the potential pain, suffering, and psychological stress of pregnancy, child-birth, and motherhood if they become pregnant and do not want a child (20)? Besides, once we start prohibiting women from having abortions, we will wind up telling them who they can marry and dictating the rest of their lives for them (21).

The antiabortionists have an answer for this last question. They say that the real issue centers on the fact that we are dealing with a human life. Now if fetuses really were human, I would agree that abor-tion would be murder, and I would not go so far as to say that murder should take priority over the wishes of the mother. The proof that this is not so, though, consists in the fact that they can't tell us when human life really begins (22). Some say at the time of conception. Others say at three months, and still others at birth. Thus we see the choice is arbitrary (23). Personally, I think life begins when the child could begin breathing and be independent of the mother (24). At any rate, the antiabortionists have no better reasons for thinking abortion is murder than I do for thinking it is not. So abortion is morally right (25).

Comments

1. This and similar types of opening sentences ought to be avoided. They are not necessary, have a hollow ring to them, and often appear as attempts to convince the reader of the importance of the prob-lem being dealt with.

2. Abortion itself is not *a* question much less *the* question "What is right?" or "What is wrong?" Rather, it is an action. Moreover, even if abortions were performed five thousand years ago, there is some doubt about whether they posed any particular moral issue.

3. Autobiographical references should be avoided unless they provide useful information relevant to one's case. Any reader will assume that the case being argued "seems" to the writer to be true.

4. This claim should have been immediately clarified, so that the reader would know exactly what is being asserted and be able to assess the soundness of its supporting arguments. As stated, it might mean anything from "Abortion is always justified for any reason whatsoever, even as an alternative to birth control" to "Abortion is justified only when the life of the mother is at stake." The problem is not clearly trans-lated into a statement of a specific issue.

5. This is a good example of the fallacy of irrelevant reasons (non sequitur), since it presents a Supreme Court decision as evidence for the

morality of a practice. But when the Supreme Court pronounces on the constitutionality of an issue, it is still open to question whether it is moral. Legal justification and moral justification are not the same thing.

6. Question-begging definitions should always be avoided. Here "thinking person" has been redefined so as to include only those people who agree with the author on this issue.

7. No one denies that we are entitled to our own philosophical opinions in the sense of exercising a right to have an opinion. Hence, this clause is not worth including.

8. This statement is superfluous, since the purpose of any philosophy essay is to convince others with arguments. Also, this qualification may just imply that the writer wants to be excused from arguing a case on the mistaken assumption that philosophical commitment is arbitrary. The entire introductory paragraph leaves much to be desired. We are presented with only vague ideas of the problem and of what the author intends to show, with no indication of how the author intends to proceed. In general, then, the paragraph fails to conform adequately to the principles of good introduction set forth earlier in this chapter.

9. This sentence appears from out of nowhere, with no forewarning or transitional elements to help the reader place in perspective the relevance of religion for the issue of abortion. Use of the term "influence" suggests the writer is concerned with the psychological or sociological effect of certain religious ideas. In fact, it is the logical or conceptual relevance of these ideas that is at stake. For example, the basic claim of this paragraph is that the antiabortion position is based upon certain false religious assumptions. Yet the distinction between assumptions that serve as necessary conditions and those that serve as sufficient conditions is particularly important here. The assumption the writer cites, belief in souls, is certainly not a necessary condition of the belief in the immorality of abortion. Yet in apparently rejecting that assumption, the writer implies that the antiabortion view must also collapse. This would be an effective strategy only if the assumption were a necessary condition.

10. It is unlikely that the writer intends to say that a preoccupation with the soul leads to (causes) an otherworldly orientation since this preoccupation is but one of many manifestations of an already established otherworldly orientation. The author's meaning and the meaning of the word "lead" do not harmonize. Moreover, this is but one of several rather lengthy and poorly executed sentences in the draft. The sentence might better be broken down and presented as follows: "The orientation of religion tends to generate an insensitive attitude towards pressing contemporary moral issues, such as abortion. Those persons more concerned with the soul are less likely to take seriously the problems of unwanted children." (Of course, whether this is true is another issue.)

11. It is usually prudent to avoid rhetorical questions in philosophy essays and say what is on one's mind. This question might better be reformulated as follows: "Consider, for example, the fact of thousands of unwanted children growing up undernourished, poorly educated, or at best unloved and uncared for."

12. Leading questions should always be avoided, and nothing would be lost by deleting this sentence. Clearly, what often happens to unwanted children is not good.

13. Again, there is no transition or forewarning. The writer should take one argument at a time and not introduce new issues until ready to deal with them. A "drifting" phenomenon is evident. Moreover, this way of stating the matter suggests that the writer assumes without question that the fetus is nothing more than a (disposable?) "part" of the mother's body on a par with, say, a finger.

14. Which point is at issue here? Several are mentioned in the preceding paragraph. Moreover, we recall that examples exemplify. They do not prove claims. "Prove" should be changed to "illustrate."

15. This poorly expressed sentence contains several questionable claims and assumptions that do not receive adequate critical attention. Which society are we talking about? Is, say, American culture "filled" with religious beliefs and attitudes? Is fear of God representative of them? Who is being blamed—society, religion, or both? Or should we also blame Mary to some extent for being so influenced by what others think? Moreover, the writer assumes without argument that the religious beliefs in question are false. It is also assumed that Mary ought not to feel guilty about possibly having an abortion. If so, why? The feeling alone doesn't prove anything one way or the other.

16. Several additional comments about this paragraph are in order. To begin, unless this illustration is supposed to be a unique case, it is drawn out in unnecessary detail. The general problem of unwanted children can be illustrated specifically by citing a broader range of reasons for not wanting children; discussion might include, for example, abortion of fetuses with probable physical or mental defects. Secondly, the writer does not come to grips with the new issue, namely, under what circumstances, if any, not wanting a child is sufficient to justify its early extinction. In the present paragraph the writer merely tells us a story and assumes the case is established. A "drifting" phenomenon is again evident. Finally, the point concerning the child's retardation is a red herring. Wanted as well as unwanted children can be retarded, and so the pity that is evoked by citing the retardation is a diversion from the issue of abortion. It should be eliminated.

17. Since it introduces both a new paragraph and a new "argument," this sentence should be replaced by a more relevant alternative, such as, "Let me now attempt to show how the rights of the mother are overlooked by those who favor strong restrictions on abortion."

18. This is certainly a non sequitur, with a flavor of bandwagon as well. That any number of people engage in a practice provides no evidence that it's moral (or immoral). The most that could be claimed is that more people regard abortion as moral.

19. The word 'contradiction' is often overworked in philosophy papers. It should be applied only when something is asserted both to be the case and not to be the case—which is not true in the present context. That people have some rights does not automatically entail that they should have others.

20. The lack of clarity in the introduction about exactly what the writer proposed to argue for (or against) reappears here. This sentence suggests there are good reasons for obtaining an abortion, such as the psychological instability of the mother. If so, these reasons are not spelled out in any detail. For example, how much instability is sufficient to justify abortions? But then again, the sentence might be interpreted as holding that abortions ought to be granted on demand for any reason whatsoever. Vagueness, imprecision, and ambiguity are evident.

21. This sentence provides a good illustration of the slippery slope fallacy. It should be omitted since no evidence is given that banning abortions will lead to the repressive legislation mentioned here.

22. Use of the word 'this' in this sentence has an ambiguous referent. Moreover, what is presented in this sentence is an alleged fact, not a "proof." Proofs consist of conclusions validly drawn from true premises. If an argument is intended here, as it should be, then it should be spelled out. For example:

1. If fetuses are human, then abortion is murder.
2. If life begins at conception, then fetuses are human.
3. Nobody knows when life begins.

---

4. Therefore, abortion is not murder.

Of course, this is not a valid argument. The third premise does not express the denial of the antecedent (the "if" clause) of the second premise, and even if it did, the form would still be invalid.

23. The term 'thus' suggests that an argument is being advanced here. If so, it is invalid. From people's disagreement over when human life begins, it does not follow that a given choice in the matter is arbitrary. 'Arbitrary' means 'whimsical,' 'capricious,' or 'based upon one's unsupported preference.' And surely there are better reasons than personal preference for holding that human life begins at, say, the time of conception rather than the 138th day of pregnancy (or 141st or 123rd or 130th). The passage is further complicated both by the apparent assumption that people who agree have arrived at the truth and by the possibility that the writer may have intended to say 'unproven' rather than 'arbitrary'—if the writer thought about it. Also, the claims and quasi arguments here and elsewhere in the essay are not, of course, original. Instead of simply multiplying familiar points, the writer ought to have developed fewer points in greater detail, thereby strengthening the case and exercising individual thought. The writer might have attempted, for example, to meet more objections to the essay's claims.

24. This is a good example of the writer's failure to think through the consequences of a position. For most children born at nine months could have been born at seven (six?) months, begun breathing, and become independent of the mother. Yet in the writer's view the aborting at six or seven months of a fetus that would normally be born at nine months would be fully justified. The only way this consequence can be avoided is to retract the claim that decisions of when human life begins are arbitrary. In other words, it seems inconsistent for the writer to argue in one breath that life begins at any arbitrary point and in another deny that an eight-month pregnancy should be terminated, on the grounds that at that point the fetus is a human being.

25. This conclusion is much too strong for the arguments presented. When one concludes that a certain thesis is preferable to another, one should do so because the weight of evidence favors that thesis. Yet in the preceding sentence it is asserted that the evidence doesn't favor either position. This ending exemplifies an inconsistency running throughout the essay. The writer states in some places that the whole issue boils down to a matter of arbitrarily choosing one's position yet offers "proofs" of a position in other places. In varying degrees, the author has violated all five primary rules for writing a critical philosophy essay.

Revised Draft

Although it established within broad limits the legality of obtaining an abortion, the Supreme Court ruling leaves unresolved the moral issue. Under what conditions is terminating the development of a human fetus morally justified? Although an expectant mother is now *legally* free up to a point to obtain an abortion, she may still be faced with the question of whether she *ought* to do so. In this essay I shall not attempt to determine all of the conditions under which abortion is justifiable. Rather, my purpose is essentially to criticize the thesis that abortion is never morally justified except perhaps when the life of the mother is at stake. Briefly, I shall attempt to undermine the logical relevance of certain religious beliefs for the antiabortion position. I shall also present reasons for doubting that human life begins at conception.

Let's first examine the relevance of certain religious beliefs for the issue of abortion. It is often argued that abortion is wrong because human life is sacred, and that human life is sacred because it is a "gift of God." Or it is urged that the ultimate value of human life stems from our having immaterial souls whose prime mission is to attain salvation.

My first objection to this theological basis of the antiabortion view is as follows. The beliefs that God exists, that He created us, and that we are immortal souls are most problematic. Serious doubts about their truth have been raised. We do not know whether God exists or not. Yet we do know that every year, despite their mothers' efforts to the contrary, thousands of children are conceived only to face a life of hunger, illiteracy, and poverty. When a religious belief conflicts with established facts, surely we should base our actions upon the latter. Speculation about the soul should not take precedence over the elimination of undoubtedly many future lives of misery.

My second objection is that the existence of God, the soul, and immortality is actually irrelevant to the "sacredness" of human life. If we are to locate some factor that makes life intrinsically good and the human species worth preserving, we must look to human actions, ideals, intelligence, and creative achievement. For example, if I devote my life to eradicating hunger, it may be said that I was a good person. If so, however, my goodness resides in my actions, irrespective of whether I am a soul in a body or just a physical body. To put my point differently, a soul that never did anything would be a useless lump of stuff, worth neither creating, preserving, nor destroying. Being a soul, then, is irrelevant to the value of human life.

Of course, showing the irrelevance of certain religious beliefs to the value of human life does not automatically demonstrate that abortion is morally justified. For example, an atheist may reject abortion for reasons completely independent of religion. Let us, then, consider one of those reasons, namely, the claim that human life begins with conception; we shall consider this claim in the light of its relevance to two proabortion arguments.

To begin, it is often claimed that because women have a right to control their own bodies, they should also have the right to obtain an abortion. But if human life begins with conception, then presumably fetuses have rights, too—among them the right to life. Thus the issue is not over a woman's right to control her body, but rather, over a conflict of rights. Whose rights should take precedence? Similarly, if fetuses are humans, then aborting them on the grounds that they would in all likelihood lead miserable and poverty-stricken lives would in principle be no different from killing a newborn infant for the same reasons. In both cases the crucial issue is whether fetuses are human beings.

Some fetuses must be humans, namely, those from, say, six to nine months, because many six-month fetuses are viable—they could survive independently of the mother if born prematurely. But are fetuses humans from conception onward? If not, then where shall we draw the line between human and nonhuman? I shall not attempt to draw such a line in this essay. I wish only to show that there are reasons for doubting that human life extends all the way to conception. It is therefore reasonable to suppose that there is *some* period between conception and birth in which we may be justified in saying that fetuses are not human. I shall present two arguments.

First, the organism at four weeks from conception has neither the form nor the function of a human being. Indeed, at this stage it is indistinguishable from the fetus of a monkey. More specifically, brain-wave activity does not begin until quite some time after conception; exactly when is a matter for biologists to determine. And since a lack of such activity is the criterion of death, then its beginning in the human fetus should be the criterion of life's having begun.

Second, in the case of twins the twinning process does not take place until about six weeks after conception. Thus, even if we suppose that human life begins in general at six weeks, it cannot be claimed coherently that I as a twin, for example, existed prior to that time. To be sure, one of the causes of my coming into being existed prior to that time, but not *I*. There appear to be reasons, therefore, for doubting that conception is the beginning of human life. We may conclude that, contrary to the extreme antiabortion position, there are some circumstances in which abortion might be morally justified. Exactly what those circumstances are and where we should draw the line are topics for another essay.

Answers to Exercises

What Kind of Claim Is
Advanced? (p. 55)

A. 1. This is an empirical claim. If it is intended to be applicable to all people, it is most likely false. It is of no philosophical interest.

2. This assertion is probably intended as an analytic claim implying the logical exclusiveness of 'happiness' and 'exclusive self-concern'. If so, the 'cannot' would mean "logically cannot" in the sense that we cannot find a square circle. It might be interpreted as an empirical claim if it were falsifiable. But such claims are usually intended to assert something stronger, i.e., a necessary truth that cannot be overturned by empirical fact.

3. The term 'basis' is ambiguous. It may imply an empirical claim about causes; that is, the desire to be happy is what allegedly causes a person to develop moral standards. Or it may imply a normative thesis about how moral judgments should be justified; that is, an adequate moral standard must judge rightness and wrongness in relation to the happiness produced by an action. The latter sense is philosophically interesting. It suggests a definition of 'right action' as "an action that produces happiness."

4. This claim expresses the special kind of necessary truth called a tautology. It is true of anything. For example, all cars are either Chevrolets or non-Chevrolets. It is neither empirically nor philosophically controversial.

5. This claim is definitional (although it is a poor definition).

B. 1. This question is empirical and invites a straightforward answer, e.g., "It is now 10:00 A.M."

2. This question expresses a request for a definition of time. Definitions are a type of analytic proposition.

3. This question expresses a request for a consequence of our understanding of the meaning of time. To answer it would be to clarify our understanding of the concept of time. While some implied definition of time may be in the background, a definition per se is not being requested. The answer would involve an a priori claim of the analytic variety.

4. This question simply requests a personal reaction regarding what you take to be the case. It is empirical.

5. This question is normative. It has a prescriptive, guiding function. It is not primarily a request for information.

C. 1. This claim is advanced as a necessarily true proposition of an analytic variety. It asserts a logical or conceptual incompatibility between 'existentialists' and 'philosophers' based on certain presumed meanings of those terms. It has the same form as "Jane can't be a Marxist because she believes in the free-enterprise system."

2. This claim is purely definitional; it asserts that "love of wisdom" is an analytic consequence of 'philosophy' (which, you recall, meant "love of wisdom" in ancient Greece).

3. This is certainly a necessary (a priori) claim.

4. This is a straightforward empirical claim.

5. This is probably intended as an empirical claim that, as a matter of observable fact, philosophers just haven't solved any pressing moral, social, or political issues in recent times. Alternatively, it might be intended as a stronger, a priori claim that philosophy by its very nature cannot resolve such issues.

D. 1. This is a straightforward empirical claim (and true).

2. This is a normative (moral) claim about what the speaker believes *ought* to be the case.

3. This is an a priori claim about what conceptually *must* be the case, given the overlapping definitions of each.

4. Some religious scholars dispute this, but the average person believes the two to be *necessarily* different. Hence, an a priori claim is being made.

5. This, too, is an a priori claim. It does not just happen to be true, but must be true, given the definition of Judaism.

E. 1. This claim is possibly definitional; it offers a rather narrow description of a male chauvinist. It may also be interpreted as giving one (of several possible) analytic consequence of someone's being a male chauvinist.

2. This claim is straightforwardly definitional.

3. This may be interpreted as an a priori claim necessarily (though nondefinitionally) linking ideas of "immoral sex" and "irresponsible participants." In other words, responsible behavior by the partners is asserted to be a necessary condition of moral sex. For this reason, it may also be interpreted as a normative claim, which prescribes in effect: "Only engage in responsible sex."

4. The 'can't' in this sentence may be interpreted as an empirical claim that puritanical persons just cannot bring themselves to enjoy sex. Or it may be interpreted as a logical (a priori) claim that inability to enjoy sex is part of the meaning of 'puritan'.

5. This claim is analytically (necessarily) true because "too much" of anything is abnormal.

F. 1. This claim is empirical and probably true.

2. This claim is a priori of an analytic variety. It asserts that part of the meaning of democracy is such that, necessarily, we must permit it to self-destruct at the hands of the majority.

3. This is another analytic (a priori) claim, asserting that free choice must be part of our understanding of the concept of democracy.

4. This claim has both normative and empirical elements. On the one hand, it seems to assert that the correctability of leaders' mistakes is a "good thing," an ideal to which we ought to commit ourselves. On the other hand, it is a simple fact that such correctability has made it possible to reach universal human goals that might be ruled out in dictatorships. We might even turn it into an a priori claim that asserts that such correctability is part of the very meaning of democracy. Without a fuller context, it is often difficult to decide what type of claim is intended.

5. This is an empirical claim, probably true.

What Is the Meaning of Key Terms? (p. 67)

A. Lots of persons may know of events coming up in your future on empirical grounds. The definition says nothing about how the psychic knows your future.

B. In times past, many persons felt that segregated schools were morally permissible. Yet surely this is wrong. Hence, morality cannot be entirely dependent on what persons happen to believe at any given time.

C. Day precedes (as well as follows) night, yet it does not cause the occurrence of night.

D. This definition assumes that philosophy is a kind of "pre-science" and that in principle science is capable of answering the questions philosophers raise. This assumption is mistaken (see p. 11). For example, scientific method is not capable of telling us whether minority "quotas" are morally justifiable.

E. This claim is countered with the fact that many "nice guys" finish last.

F. Good teachers must also be able to explain effectively what they know.

G. Many beliefs held strongly and sincerely nevertheless turn out to be false—for example, the old belief that the earth is the center of the universe. If something is known, it must be true as well as believed. Can you think of any other conditions?

H. There are potentially true beliefs ("There used to be many dinosaurs in this state") with no workable implications, in a normal sense of 'workable', and there are many beliefs that may work for the individual ("I believe in the existence of a supreme being") yet may not be true.

I. The 1954 Supreme Court case of *Brown v. The Board of Education* is certainly an example of justice and not of paying off one's friends.

J. Respect is a part of love, but they are not the same. I may respect you but not love you.

K. A misstatement would normally be interpreted as unintentional, such as a slip of the tongue. Lies are intentional. A dozen or more examples of the difference should come to mind.

L. Feminists are often concerned with issues that go beyond equality between the sexes, such as hierarchical power structures.

M. Some UFOs may well have been built by humans here on Earth.

Do the Arguments Support the Thesis? (p. 75)

A. This argument is invalid. It commits a fallacy called "denying the antecedent." This form is always fallacious:

> If p, then q
> Not p
> _____
> Therefore, not q

B. This argument is valid. Its logical form is:

> If p then q
> If q, then not r
> But r
> _____
> Therefore, not p

This inference reflects a double application of the *modus tollens* pattern. From the second and third premises alone we could derive not q, and when we apply not q to the first premise, we then derive not p.

C. This argument is invalid. It commits a fallacy called "affirming the consequent." This form is always fallacious:

> If p, then q
> q
> _____
> Therefore, p

D. This argument is valid. The first premise is a tautology, and it is logically unnecessary for deriving the stated conclusion. The conclusion can be derived by a *modus tollens* operation on the second and third premises. Its form is:

> p or not p
> If p, then not q
> But q
> _____
>
> Therefore, not p

(Note: What is critical about the *modus tollens* forms that are contained in this argument and in B above is that one premise is a denial of the consequent of the other. It does not matter which is stated in the affirmative and which in the negative, so long as there is one affirmative and one negative.)

E. This argument is valid. It corresponds to the *modus ponens* argument.

F. This argument illustrates a different kind of deductive logic, one based on class relationships rather than on relations between simple propositions. Its form is:

Some s are p		Some s are p
All q are not p	← or →	No q are p
_____		
No q are s		No q are s

For reasons we cannot elaborate upon here, strict logical form requires that we translate the second premise as indicated in the right-hand argument. "No q are p" is the preferred way of stating "All q are not p." The argument is invalid. Given the premises, it turns out that some defenders of civil liberties could still be biologists.

Are the Assumptions Correct? (p. 80)

A. One questionable assumption is that the exclusive cause of all criminal acts is environmental rather than genetic—that there are no "born" criminals.

B. This assumes that having an original copy of one's birth certificate plus newspapers of the time marking the event (which Obama did) is not sufficient to demonstrate that one was born where he says he was.

C. A questionable assumption is that physical maturity implies intellectual and, in particular, political maturity.

D. This abbreviated argument appears to work only if we assume that the fetus is a "part" of a woman's body in the same sense that her other "parts" are, such as fingers or kidneys (which clearly she does have the right to remove).

E. This claim falsely assumes that correlation is the same as identity—that X must be Y if the two are always found together.

F. This claim assumes that, given enough time, truth wins out, which is not always so.

G. A questionable assumption of this passage is that to truly appreciate and understand something one must have directly experienced it from the "inside."

H. This claim assumes that science is the kind of discipline that could do this, when in fact scientific method does not include within its scope the testability of religious faith.

I. This claim falsely assumes that voting is the only way to bring about a desired change. It might also be effective to abstain from voting or just to campaign in large numbers.

J. This claim assumes that more lives would be saved with nuclear weapons than through conventional warfare. (This may have been a reasonable assumption, even if not correct. At the time there were many unknown variables.)

K. This assumes that the values of the majority ought to be everyone's values.

L. This claim makes several questionable assumptions, among them that freedom and predictability (the cornerstone of a science of human behavior assumed by behaviorists) are incompatible.

M. This claim assumes we know what "perfect" means in this context and that it is desirable to act on this assumption.

Are the Logical Consequences Plausible? (p. 84)

A. Since this statement is itself a generalization, then it must be false also. Hence, it is self-refuting.

B. If everyone lied, the distinction between truth and falsehood would be called into question, one possible extreme outcome being that lies would no longer be lies.

C. This proposal would yield the false consequence that no person could ever behave as though depressed yet actually feel happy, for there would be no difference between feeling and behaving.

D. Were this the case, then communication would be seriously jeopardized.

E. … then, if murder is a prosecutable offense, both women and their doctors should be prosecuted to some degree.

F. If so, then how would we know that "regular" unconstructed persons were conscious beings?

G. Without certain qualifications, this prescription is self-defeating in a practical sense. For example, it may be in someone's self-interest to kill the person who makes the prescription. And this consequence is not in the latter person's interest.

H. Depending on how broadly "hazardous" is interpreted, we might be forced to pass laws against almost everything since most of life carries some degree of risk. Pushed to the extreme, we might not even be able to enjoy our health without violating the law.

I. If pornography is censored today, then what about artistic representations of sex tomorrow and so on, ad infinitum, on the grounds that some group finds them distasteful?

J. This claim overlooks the rights of any given minority. Suppose the "majority" voted to extinguish all Chinese Americans?

K. Then we presumably have no way to know that others even have experiences, much less what they are like.

L. Jesus, among others. But surely he was successful, if not deeply satisfied with his work.

M. Carried to its extreme, this adage implies that we can never really find happiness, success, and the like, for as soon as we arrive on the other side, it no longer looks so good. Greener pastures are always on the other side.

N. Then we would all, in some special sense, be conformists. The thesis is self-defeating.

O. There is an internal contradiction here. Perhaps one ought not attend the rodeo on the grounds that horses are not treated very "humanely."

How Adequate Is the Theory? (p. 87)

A. Many people have a very strong will to do something—for example, to overcome an addiction to heroin—yet are unable to do so. You should resist the temptation to interpret the platitude in exercise A as completely nonfalsifiable, making it immune to counterexample; you should not suppose that whenever someone tries but fails, he or she hasn't really tried hard enough.

B. This overlooks one important goal of clinical psychology, namely, helping persons through therapy.

C. This conception of the purpose of dramatic acting is extremely narrow. One might just as easily suppose that the purpose of acting is to convey a theme or message or even to bring pleasure to the actors themselves.

D. Given the normal sense of 'pleasure', we would say that many other things might be central goals in life, such as fulfilling one's obligations and finding peace of mind. (Note: Some of you will no doubt want to expand the concept of pleasure to include succeeding in anything one sets out to do. You will probably discuss the problems with this approach in class.)

E. If carried out to a significant degree, this implied theory of government might cause our current government to collapse.

F. This account of the difference between philosophy and science is inadequate both because science does sometimes deal with unobservable entities and because philosophy certainly concerns itself with the interpretation of things that can be seen.

G. This statement suggests not only that practical knowledge is necessary for the educated person but perhaps also that it is the only— or at least the most important—type of knowledge to have. To restrict the importance of theoretical education in this way seems unnecessarily arbitrary, as well as inadequate.

H. Everything depends upon the context here. Sometimes, for example, staying home ("nothing") is better than, say, going out with just anybody ("something").

I. In certain contexts this may well be true. But as a universal truth it seems inadequate; for one thing, it suggests that nonlovers are fundamentally deficient and ought to improve themselves by finding someone to love.

J. Inferior in what respect? Perhaps we would have something to teach them about emotions or spirituality.

Five Common Informal Fallacies (p. 93)

A. Ad hominem
B. Straw man
C. Slippery slope
D. Question-begging definition
E. Circular argument
F. Circular argument
G. Slippery slope
H. Straw man
I. No fallacy

Appendix: Brief Synopses
of Philosophers' Thoughts

In compiling this appendix, I am deeply indebted to my colleagues in the Department of Philosophy at Georgia State University: Robert Arrington, Linda Bell, James Humber, Angel Medina, Robert Almeder, and Grant Luckhardt, and to a recent graduate, Keith Parsons. Many of the philosophers included in this survey made original contributions to areas outside of philosophy. Hence, the phrase "principal works" in some entries should be taken to include philosophical writings or works that are of some enduring interest to philosophers. In most cases, not all of their writings are included. For further authoritative overviews, consult Robert Arrington, ed. *A Companion to the Philosophers* (Malden, Ma: Blackwells, 1999).

Thales (flourished c. 585 B.C.) was one of the Seven Sages, whose sayings represented the practical wisdom of Greece. Often considered the first Western philosopher, he lived in Miletus, a Greek colonial town on the Turkish coast. No genuine fragment of his writing survives, but he is reported to have said that "Everything is full of gods," signifying a naturalistic cosmology, and that "Water is the first principle," signifying a unity behind all the diversity of things in the world.

Anaximander (c. 611–546 B.C.), a scientist and philosopher from Miletus, is often called the founder of astronomy. He was a naturalistic metaphysician who termed the primary substance from which everything is generated the "Unlimited." This term indicates that existence is not to be identified with any one known substance in the world but is a primitive unity of all substances. The process of "separation," by which things become what they are from the Unlimited, proceeds according to an order and is eternal. Any one substance always returns to the Unlimited at its destruction so that new substances may continually arise. Six fragments of Anaximander's writings survive.

Pythagoras (c. 580–500 B.C.), Ionian mathematician, philosopher, and religious leader, founded a secret fraternal society that lasted until about 300 B.C. Because of the society's commitment to secrecy, neither Pythagoras nor his followers, the Pythagoreans, left any writings. They are thought to have relied heavily on mystic insight for knowledge and to have believed that the key to understanding the universe lies in numbers, since "all is number," that is, all existing things can ultimately be reduced to ratios between whole numbers. They also apparently believed in the successive reincarnation of the soul in different species and in its liberation from the "wheel of life" through knowledge.

Gautama Siddhartha, the Buddha (c. 563–483 B.C.), of India, founded the religion and philosophy of Buddhism. Rejecting asceticism, materialism, and the ritualism of Hinduism, he achieved enlightenment in a special type of mystical experience, Nirvana. From this he stated his Four Noble Truths: (1) Life is suffering; (2) the cause of suffering is desire and attachment, from whence arises the idea of ego; (3) suffering can be overcome by severing the bonds of attachment; and (4) this can be done in turn by following the Eightfold Path. Gautama held all things to be interconnected and in a state of flux. He rejected the idea of a personal God and resisted speculation about reincarnation, although this doctrine is generally part of Buddhist religion. He left no written work, although his followers recorded and preserved his teachings.

Lao Tzu (c. sixth century B.C.) was a Chinese sage and the founder of Taoism, a religion and way of life with strong affinities to nature mysticism. In contrast to Confucianism, Lao Tzu stressed simplicity and harmony with the natural rhythms of nature. Rather than regulate perfection, he would have things evolve in their own way to their highest states. Happiness is found by living in accordance with the Tao, which is both the impersonal source of all things and nature transforming itself spontaneously. Passivity is stressed as a way of cooperating with the Tao, as is returning kindness for evil. Both are seen as forms of strength. Lao Tzu is given credit for the main ideas of the *Tao Te Ching* (*The Way of Life*), although it was probably compiled by his later followers.

Anaximenes (flourished c. 546 B.C.), a pupil of Anaximander and the third of the three "Milesian monists," believed that the essential primary substance is air. Everything in the world, including human souls and even gods, is generated from air by the processes of condensation and rarefaction.

Thus stones are extremely dense air and fire extremely rarefied air. This reduction of apparent qualitative differences in things to differences in quantity alone typifies much later scientific thought. He wrote one book, of which only references survive in the writings of later philosophers.

Confucius (551–479 B.C.), a Chinese philosopher and sage, founded the religion of Confucianism. He drew heavily from existing traditions of Chinese culture, providing a distinctive humanistic emphasis. We should strive to develop important virtues, such as moderation and self-control, and to the extent we are successful in this and in perfecting our personal relations, government by law becomes less necessary. The interaction between *jen* (human nature) and *li* (order and regulation) is the basis of much Confucian thought. Thus, human conduct is stressed in preference to the worship of anything supernatural. Principal work: *The Analects.*

Heraclitus (c. 540–480 B.C.) lived in Ephesus (in present-day Turkey) and was often called "the Obscure," presumably for his ambiguous and cryptic writing style. "Everything changes," he declared, and he used fire as a symbol of the continuous change in the universe, which is tied together in an orderly "unity of opposites." Heraclitus was perhaps the first philosopher to question the validity of sense perception. Although the unity of opposites may not be obvious to the senses, reason (*logos*) shows that the world exists as a system in which changes in one direction are always balanced by changes in another and in which opposites cannot exist without each other. Contemptuous of the masses, Heraclitus rebuked them for their lack of understanding and compared them to donkeys, which prefer chaff to gold. He wrote one long book, of which only fragments survive.

Parmenides (born c. 515 B.C.) founded the Eleatic school of philosophy in ancient southern Italy. The most rationalistic of all the monists, he believed not simply that everything is derived or generated from one substance but that everything is one and that what we take to be a multiplicity of existing things can be shown to be false by rational argument. What truly exists ("Being") is one, uncreated, indestructible, and, contrary to what Heraclitus had said, unchanging. His surviving writings come from his poem, "On Nature."

Anaxagoras (c. 500–428 B.C.) was a pluralist who differed from Empedocles in believing that the universe initially contained an infinite number of "seeds," as different from each other as the various things in the universe. Mind (*nous*) acted on these seeds, revolving them so that they began to mix together. Mind arranged the mixtures in certain ways and caused them to separate off into the various things that now exist. But because everything came from the original mixture, everything contains a portion of everything else. Anaxagoras wrote one book, untitled, of which several fragments survive.

Empedocles (c. 490–430 B.C.), a native of Sicily, was said to have been influenced by both Parmenides and Pythagoras. He was famous as an orator, a poet, a statesman, a healer who specialized in raising people from the dead, a self-styled god, and a philosopher. A pluralist, he claimed that two forces, Love and Strife, continually interact to join together and to separate the four elements of the universe, Earth, Air, Fire, and Water. Bones, for instance, are nothing but a combination of earth, water, and fire in the ratio 2:2:4. He conceived of a deity who is invisible, incorporeal, and totally nonanthropomorphic, consisting of mind alone. Only fragments remain of his two poems "On Nature" and "Purifications."

Socrates (470–399 B.C.), of Athens, forms the boundary between "pre-Socratic" and subsequent Greek philosophy. In his early life he was a courageous soldier, but he later turned from military pursuits to philosophical inquiry and social criticism. Disdainful of material goods and the ordinary conception of the good life, he took as his pursuit the love of wisdom (*sophia*)—that is, philosophy. Although he claimed that he knew only one thing—that he knew nothing—he was feared in debate for his cross-questioning of those who claimed to know and for his ability to refute rhetorical and ill-founded arguments. Charged late in his life with not believing in the state gods and with corrupting the youth, he was convicted and sentenced to death. Refusing friends' offers to assist in his escape, he stayed in jail and drank the fatal hemlock. He wrote no philosophy.

Democritus (c. 460–370 B.C.), one of the founders of Greek atomism, wrote on a wide range of topics, including physics, ethics, medicine, travel, mathematics, and botany. The fundamental thesis of atomism is that everything that exists is composed of an infinite number of tiny, indivisible, material particles, called atoms, and space. Differences between things are explained in terms of changes in the shape, motion, and position of these atoms. Matter is indestructible, and energy is conserved within the system. Democritus rejected the belief in supernatural nonmaterial beings, saying it was a result of the desire to explain terrifying natural phenomena such as thunder and lightning. Only fragments of his writings survive.

Plato (429–347 B.C.), Greek philosopher, founded his own school of philosophy in Athens, the Academy. Combining strands of thought from Heraclitus, Parmenides, and Pythagoras, Plato represented reality as twofold: the physical world, subject to change and incapable of being known, and the intelligible world, or World of Forms, which is eternal, unchanging, and knowable. The object of the philosopher is to reach this second world and thus to obtain knowledge of such entities as the form of triangles, beauty (as opposed to earthly imitations of this form), and justice (as opposed to imperfect systems such as the one that convicted Socrates). He wrote chiefly in dialogue form, and almost all of his works survive. His principal philosophical works include: *Protagoras, Gorgias, Meno, Apology, Phaedo, Crito, Republic, Parmenides, Theaetetus, Sophist, and Laws.*

Aristotle (384–322 B.C.), Greek philosopher, was at one time the outstanding student at Plato's Academy (from which he later broke and formed his own school, the Lyceum). Aristotle was sensitive to the historical development of ideas, devoted to common sense, and careful to avoid extremes in philosophy. A giant of Western thought, he mastered and improved upon most of the known disciplines of his day and made a lasting impact on both science and philosophy. His logic is still taught in universities today. In metaphysics he is noted for his rejection of the "separateness" of Plato's Forms; his analysis of matter, form, potentiality, substance, causality, and time; his doctrine of the Prime Mover; and his generally teleological world view, the impact of which is still very much felt today. In ethics and social philosophy, he is known for his defense of the "mean" in human action (where, for example, courage is the preferred middle way between rashness and cowardice), his analyses of virtue and of moral responsibility, and his emphasis on the importance of particular situations where, he urged, "the decision rests with perception." Principal philosophical works: *Metaphysics, Physics, De Anima, Nicomachean Ethics, Politics,* and *Poetics.*

Epicurus (341–270 B.C.), one of the late atomists, founded the school named after him and introduced the theory of the "swerve" into atomism in order to avoid the determinism of Democritus' system. Epicureanism as a way of life posited pleasure as the chief end of humans but recommended achieving a maximum of pleasure and a minimum of pain by suppressing one's "unnecessary" desires, cultivating friends, and ceasing to fear the gods and death. The gods exist but they are material, and in their eternal contentment are neither providential nor punishers, taking no concern for earth or its creatures. Several fragments of Epicurus' writings exist, but they are a small portion of the more than three hundred papyrus rolls he is believed to have written.

Marcus Tullius Cicero (106–43 B.C.), Roman orator and statesman, had a strong interest in philosophy and wrote a number of philosophical works. In political theory he is known for his belief in human rights and the brotherhood of man, and in ethics he was attracted by Stoic doctrines. Although he argued against Stoic fatalism, in general he adopted a stoic attitude toward theology, maintaining that it is prudent to practice traditional rites and ceremonies. Principal works: *De Republica, The Orations, De Finibus Bonorum et Malorum.*

Lucretius (c. 99–55 B.C.), a Roman philosopher, expounded and popularized the atomism of his favorite philosopher, Epicurus. He followed Epicurus in his uncompromising materialism but exceeded him with a denunciation of religion and the evils he thought it produced ("So great the evils which religion could prompt"). Principal work: *On the Nature of Things.*

Marcus Aurelius (A.D. 121–180) was emperor of Rome from A.D. 161 to 180 and was one of the late Stoic philosophers. His only extant work is a collection of aphorisms and reflections that generally indicate the Stoic influence of Epictetus. Some of the more important of these doctrines are: individual self-sufficiency in the face of adversity, the cosmos as a unity governed by an intelligence, the triviality of the physical world, and the necessity of duty (as opposed to self-interest). Principal work: *Meditations.*

Plotinus (205–270), an Egyptian philosopher who later moved to Rome, is considered the greatest of the Neo-Platonists. He held that reality arises from a single ineffable and transcendent source, which he called The One. The One is beyond being, but all beings are generated out of The One through a process of "emanation." The first emanation is Mind (*nous*). The second emanation is the World-Soul, from which all individual human souls derive. The third emanation—at the greatest remove from The One—is matter. Plotinus was a mystic and viewed human salvation as liberation of the soul from the bondage of matter and the achievement of reunion with The One. Principal work: *The Enneads.*

Saint Augustine (354–430), a North African, was generally considered the first great Christian philosopher. He viewed God as the supreme being who created all things out of nothing; even time did not exist before the creation. Evil, however, was not created by God since evil does not really exist but is only a lack or privation of good. Human knowledge, since it involves knowledge of eternal truths, can only come about through a direct illumination of the mind by God. God created humans as free agents, but since the fall of Adam, humans are only free to sin if God's grace restores the power to do good. Augustine viewed the course of history as the struggle between the City of God and the City of the World, that is, between those who love God and those who love the world. Principal works: *Confessions, The City of God, On the Trinity.*

Avicenna (980–1037), known in the Middle East as Ibn Sina, was the most prominent Islamic philosopher and physician of medieval times. He made notable contributions to the fields of natural science, metaphysics, theology, and medical theory. His philosophy was Aristotelian and neo-Platonist, positing an "active intellect" capable of distinguishing a hierarchical set of realms, starting with the world of unchanging ideas and descending to the worlds of souls, physical forces, and corporeal matter. His medical theories were studied for centuries and some, such as his recognition of the effects of psychology and environment on health, remain relevant today. Many of his encyclopedic works influenced later philosophers including Averroës (Ibn Rushd), Saint Thomas Aquinas, and Henry of Ghent. Principal works: *Kitab al-Shifa (The Book of Healing), Al-Qanun fi-l-Tibb (The Canon of Medicine).*

Saint Anselm (1033–1109), English philosopher and theologian in the Augustinian tradition, is noted mainly as the formulator of the "ontological argument" for the existence of God. This argument begins with the definition of 'God' as "the greatest conceivable being" and concludes that this being must exist; otherwise it would be possible to think of another greater being—namely one that does exist. This argument, following in the Neo-Platonic tradition, assumes that absolute perfection entails existence. Anselm was Archbishop of Canterbury for sixteen years. Principal works: *Proslogion, Monologion.*

Saint Thomas Aquinas (1225–1274), Italian philosopher and theologian, is generally considered the most important medieval mind. He sought to construct a great synthesis of Aristotelian and Christian thought in which the truths of faith and the truths of reason supplement and support one another. He is most famous for his "Five Ways" of proving the existence of God. Although God's existence can thus be proven, His attributes cannot be known directly but can only be partially grasped through the application of analogies. In metaphysics Aquinas distinguished sharply between a thing's essence (what it is) and its existence (the fact that it is). He held that human laws should ultimately be grounded in eternal law—the rules whereby Divine Reason governs the universe. Principal works: *Summa Theologica, Summa Contra Gentiles.*

John Duns Scotus (1266–1308) was a Scottish philosopher and theologian whose ability to draw critical distinctions earned him the title of "The Subtle Doctor." Against Aquinas, he asserted the primacy of will in both God and man. He argued that through reason one can both prove the existence of God and know His attributes without employing analogies. Reason cannot, however, explain God's purposes or demonstrate the soul's immortality. Ethical rules, he urged, are not intrinsically good but good because they are willed by God. The American pragmatist Charles Peirce once described Scotus as one of the "profoundest metaphysicians that ever lived." Principal works: *Opera Omnia* (collected works), *A Tract Concerning the First Principle*.

William of Ockham (1285–1349), English logician and theologian, is most noted for his wide and sometimes heretical application of "Ockham's Razor," the principle that what can be explained on fewer principles is explained needlessly by more. He defended nominalism, the view that universals such as straightness or goodness are not abiding essences of things but rather are mere names for similar traits of things. He wrote widely on many subjects of varying interest. Principal works: *Commentary on the Sentences of Peter Lombard, Summa Logicae.*

Francis Bacon (1561–1626), a British empiricist, urged that "knowledge is power" and sharply criticized the abstract theorizing of the medievals. The path to knowledge is through observing nature and by applying his version of inductive method, which, it turned out, vastly underestimated the importance of mathematics and of hypothesis formulation. In studying nature, he argued, we are often misled by false ideas and methods that he labeled the "Idols" of the Tribe, the Cave, the Market Place, and the Theater. Bacon founded the Royal Society, the most prestigious scientific association in Britain and the first to emphasize the importance of science as a systematic inquiry. Principal works: *Novum Organum, The Advancement of Learning.*

Thomas Hobbes (1588–1679) was a British empiricist and materialist. According to Hobbes, only bodies exist, and the principal property shared by all bodies is motion. All thoughts are motions in bodies, and by studying bodies' motions we understand reality. (This stress on motion led some to call Hobbes a "motion-intoxicated man.") Sometimes referred to as the "father of modern totalitarianism," Hobbes felt that humans are naturally selfish beings who in theory would live in a state of "war of all against all" until they enter civil society by means of a social contract. The sovereign who enforces the contract is not party to it. Religion must be state controlled. Principal works: *Leviathan, De Cive, De Corpore, De Homine.*

René Descartes (1596–1650), French rationalist, is often referred to as the "father of modern philosophy." He sought to develop a philosophical method that would guarantee absolutely certain knowledge about the world. He insisted that *cogito ergo sum* ("I think therefore I am") is the most certain of all philosophical principles and used it as a foundation to defend dualism (the idea that mind and body are different kinds of things) and interactionism (the idea that mind and body cause changes in each other). His rationalism and dualism had a profound influence on later modern philosophy. A great mathematician, he developed analytic geometry. Principal works: *Meditations on First Philosophy, Discourse on Method, Principles of Philosophy.*

Benedictus Spinoza (1632–1677), a Jewish rationalist born in Holland, sought certainty by using a "geometric" philosophical method. (This method begins with self-evident truths and then deduces absolutely certain theorems from those truths.) He accepted monism (reality is "one") and pantheism (God is the totality of everything that is). In Spinoza's system, only God is free, and although God (Nature or the Universe as a whole) is one, this Being has two separate attributes or essences—thought and extension—which proceed along parallel courses. Spinoza accepted a teleological ethics and held that the highest human good lay in understanding one's place in the universe. Principal works: *The Ethics, On the Improvement of Human Understanding, Treatise on Theology and Politics.*

John Locke (1632–1704) was a British empiricist who held that the mind can only know its own ideas. He argued that at birth the mind is a "blank tablet," devoid of all ideas. Using what he called the "historical plain method" he sought to trace all ideas to their origins in sensation (experience of the material world) and reflection (experience of the mind's own activities, e.g., judging). His empiricism influenced later empiricists such as Berkeley and Hume. Locke was a staunch defender of democracy, and the essentials of his political theory are embodied in the U.S. Constitution and Declaration of Independence. Principal works: *An Essay Concerning Human Understanding, Two Treatises of Civil Government.*

Nicholas Malebranche (1638–1715), a French rationalist, sought to synthesize the philosophy of Descartes and the thought of Saint Augustine. He accepted dualism but rejected interactionism, arguing instead for occasionalism. He held that the mind can perceive no necessary connections between causes and effects in nature because God is the true cause of everything, and natural causes are not real causes but mere "occasions" for God's causal activity (e.g., pain is not caused by a pinprick but by God on the occasion of the prick). Malebranche's contention that natural causes and effects are not connected influenced Hume's causal theory. Principal works: *Of the Search for Truth, Elucidations on the Search for Truth, Conversations on Metaphysics.*

Gottfried Leibniz (1646–1716) was a German rationalist who tried to reconcile teleology and mechanism. He held that reality is composed of an infinite number of units of force (monads), which are "windowless" (unable to affect one another) "living mirrors" (organized in a preestablished harmony so that each monad's actions harmonize with, or reflect, the actions of all other monads). Monads act from internal causes, and these causes have the principle of sufficient reason (God and His desire to create the best of all possible worlds) as their final cause. Leibniz held that evil's existence is compatible with the idea of an all-good God because the best of all possible worlds may contain imperfection. Working independently of Newton, he developed calculus. Principle works: *New Essays on Human Understanding, Monadology, Essays in Theodicy.*

George Berkeley (1685–1753), Bishop in the Church of England, was an empiricist and a subjective idealist. Arguing that *esse est percipi* ("to be is to be perceived"), he held that the objects of perception are not material substances but rather "ideas" or collections of sensations that cannot exist apart from their being perceived (e.g., an apple is nothing more than the sensations of red, round, sweet, etc., unified in a single "complex idea"). Since matter is not perceived, it does not exist. Minds cannot be perceived, but they must exist to cause ideas. Reality is composed of finite minds, God's mind, and the contents of those minds. Human minds create imagined ideas; perceived ideas (ideas of "real" objects) are perceptions in the mind of God that He communicates to us. Principal works: *A Treatise Concerning the Principles of Human Knowledge, Three Dialogues Between Hylas and Philonous.*

Francois-Marie Arouet de Voltaire (1694–1778) was a French philosopher and novelist identified with the Enlightenment. He is remembered today primarily for his attack on philosophical optimism, in particular Leibniz's claim that this is "the best of all possible worlds." In his own time, he was known for his mocking attacks on the Catholic Church, ecclesiastics, Christian doctrines, and fanaticism and for his campaigns for social and judicial reform. A deist, he argued for the existence of God by comparing the world to a watch: since the latter is clearly made by someone for a purpose, so ought we to conclude is the former. He believed in a "general providence" and maintained that prayers cannot alter the immutable laws of the universe or prevent suffering. Principal works: *Philosophical Dictionary, Treatise on Metaphysics, Candide.*

David Hume (1711–1776), a Scottish empiricist and skeptic, held that all ideas originate from impressions (immediate perceptions). Since we have no impression of any necessary connection linking causes and effects, we do not know that fire must be hot, only that fire and heat have been constantly conjoined in the past. Without knowledge of causal necessity we have no rational justification for inferring that the future will be like the past (the problem of induction). He also claimed that we have no impression of the self, that we do not know whether matter exists, and that we cannot prove God's existence. He influenced thinkers as diverse as Kant and Einstein. Principal works: *A Treatise of Human Nature, An Enquiry Concerning Human Understanding, Principles of Morals, Dialogues Concerning Natural Religion.*

Jean-Jacques Rousseau (1712–1778), French philosopher, political theorist, and novelist, contrasted the artificiality, hypocrisy, and deceit of contemporary society with the virtue, simplicity, openness, and innocence of the primitive state of the "noble savage." He presented society as being frequently little more than an attempt to secure liberty by accepting chains and substituting moral or political inequality for natural or physical inequality. In the social contract, each citizen ideally would transfer all his rights to the community or the "general will," a common will tending to the preservation and welfare of the whole and of every part. Activity in accordance with this will is just. Principal works: *Discourse on the Origin and Foundation of the Inequality Among Men, Emile.*

Immanuel Kant (1724–1804) was a German philosopher who produced a synthesis of rationalism and empiricism often called the "Copernican Revolution" in philosophy. He argued that the mind is active in perception (it "filters" raw data) and that this action helps create the world we experience and know (phenomenal reality). Because the mind helps create phenomenal reality, we can know, prior to experience, that this reality must have certain characteristics (i.e., we have knowledge that is both synthetic and a priori, such as "All events are caused"). Things in themselves, independent of experience, cannot be known. In ethics Kant was a deontologist who held that our duty is to follow those principles that can be universally applied to all rational beings without contradiction. Principal works: *Critique of Pure Reason, Critique of Practical Reason, Critique of Judgment, Principles of the Metaphysics of Ethics.*

G. W. F. Hegel (1770–1831), the German philosopher who developed the position known as **absolute idealism,** argued that "the real is the rational" and that Reason is the formative principle of all reality. We need not be restricted, as Kant held, to the realm of mere appearances (phenomenal world). The goal of history is the liberation of Spirit (consciousness) from its confinement in nature in order to achieve the "Absolute," an all-encompassing, self-conscious, organic unity. The individual as individual is unimportant. Hegel is noted for his dialectical analyses of history and ideas, in which he traces the ways an earlier position or institution is undermined and leads beyond itself to a new synthesis. Thus, for example, master and slave may each derive some value from their relationship (each depending upon the other), but the institution of slavery itself inevitably must give way to a higher phase of historical development, reflecting the unfolding of consciousness through history. Principal works: *Phenomenology of Spirit, Philosophy of Right, Science of Logic, Encyclopaedia of the Philosophical Sciences.*

Arthur Schopenhauer (1788–1860) was a German idealist noted for his pessimistic view of life, his stipulation of the will to live as a fundamental reality, and his almost unprecedented misogynist attack on women. Caught in the will to live, we spend our lives cast back and forth between painful wants and freedom from pain, which is then attended by boredom. While reason normally serves this blind and restless will, it may turn away and engage in aesthetic contemplation. In moments of such contemplation we are truly free. All phenomena, including the human body, are but a kind of "objectified will." Schopenhauer was one of the first, and few, Western philosophers to be influenced by Eastern thought, particularly that of the Upanishads. Principal works: *The World as Will and Idea, On the Will in Nature, On the Freedom of the Will, The Two Main Problems of Ethics.*

John Stuart Mill (1806–1873), English economist, philosopher of logic and science, and ethical theorist, is particularly well known for his development and advocacy of utilitarianism in ethics. He disagreed with other utilitarians by considering the quality as well as the quantity of pleasurable and painful consequences. A great and effective spokesman for the liberal point of view, Mill argued for liberty, maintaining that "the sole end for which mankind are warranted, individually or collectively, in interfering with the liberty of any of their number, is self-protection." He was an outspoken feminist, arguing against legal and social restrictions on women. Principal works: *Utilitarianism, On Liberty, A System of Logic, The Subjection of Women, The Principles of Political Economy.*

Soren Kierkegaard (1813–1855) was a Danish philosopher generally considered to be the father of existentialism. Against mass movements, universal truth that applies to everybody and yet to nobody in particular, and the Hegelian systematic philosophy that has no room for the thinker as an individual, he held that the most difficult task facing each person is that of becoming an individual. Objective discussion inevitably misses the truth about the individual. To be an individual is to recognize one's uniqueness, to face the necessity of decision, and ultimately to take the "leap of faith." Like Abraham, the believer accepts and stands ready to act on principles and claims that may be absurd to human reason. Principal works: *Concluding Unscientific Postscript, Either/or, Fear and Trembling, The Sickness unto Death, Stages on Life's Way.*

Karl Marx (1818–1883) was the German philosopher, economist, and revolutionary who, with Friedrich Engels, founded the "leftist" tradition in political thought. Marx combined aspects of Hegel's dialectic with Feuerbach's atheistic materialism, arguing that only through a revolution of the working class could persons become truly emancipated. His early works reflect a deep concern with the dehumanizing effects of industrialization. With the revolution ideally comes a classless society, the replacement of private property with communal ownership, and the withering away of the state. Principal works: *Economic and Philosophic Manuscripts of 1844, Capital, The Communist Manifesto.*

Charles Peirce (1839–1914), distinguished mathematician and scientist, is generally regarded as the "Father of American Philosophy" and as the founder of the school of (what he termed) pragmaticism. Peirce urged that "there is no difference of meaning so fine as to consist in anything but a difference of practice." He applied this pragmatic theory of meaning largely to scientific and practical endeavors and argued that science offers the only proper method for acquiring knowledge about the world. He stressed that all of our beliefs are basically fallible and thus subject to revision in the light of incomplete and changing bodies of evidence. He published little in his lifetime. However, his works may be found in the eight-volume series *The Collected Papers of Charles Peirce.*

William James (1842–1910), American psychologist and philosopher, defended and made popular the philosophy of **pragmatism,** especially in the areas of morality and religious belief. If the psychological, moral, and/or social consequences of a belief are good, the belief counts as rational, even though it cannot be proven by science. Though it is subject to misinterpretation, he once urged that "the true is only the expedient in our way of thinking, just as the right is only the expedient in our way of behaving," that is, truth depends upon the workability of our beliefs. James had a long-standing interest in psychic phenomena, which he examined carefully in order to determine whether there is personal survival after death. Principal works: *The Principles of Psychology, Varieties of Religious Experience, The Will to Believe and Other Essays, Pragmatism, The Meaning of Truth.*

Friedrich Nietzsche (1844–1900), German philosopher, is generally regarded as an existentialist because of his emphasis on the individual and his rejection of the masses and of any views of truth and value that would camouflage the role of choice in their creation. He proposed that the fundamental metaphysical principle is the will to power and that there have been two sorts of values—those created by the weak ("slave morality") and used to enhance the power of the weak by extolling virtues such as pity, love, altruism, and meekness; and those of the strong ("master morality") with virtues such as strength and courage. Nietzsche's "Overman" would raise himself above the egalitarianism, mediocrity, nihilism, and resentment of "the herd." Beyond good and evil, the Overman would create his own values that affirm life. Nietzsche explicitly objected to anti-Semites and to those he called "scholarly oxen" for interpreting the Overman as a biological category. Principal works: *Beyond Good and Evil, Human, All-Too-Human, The Gay Science, Thus Spake Zarathustra, The Twilight of the Idols, Ecce Homo, The Will to Power.*

Francis Herbert Bradley (1846–1924) was a British idealist who, like Hegel, believed in the existence of an absolute, free from all contradictions. Unlike Hegel, Bradley believed that thought is unable to grasp ultimate reality. Yet prior to the emergence of distinctions, for example, between a thing and its properties, we have an immediate experience, a feeling-experience of "a many felt in one." By analogy with such immediate experience, we can conceive in a limited way of the absolute. Rejecting with Hegel the empty formalism of the Kantian "good will," Bradley identified the good will with the universal will, the will of the social organism. Thus, "my station and its duties" supply content for my moral life. Principal works: *Ethical Studies, The Principles of Logic, Appearance and Reality, Essays on Truth and Reality.*

Josiah Royce (1855–1916), American idealist, taught with William James and others at Harvard University's philosophy department during what has been called its golden period. Strongly influenced by Hegelian absolutism yet deeply sympathetic with pragmatism, Royce developed a unique blend of the two. He stressed the individualism of the human self but recognized that self is part of a wider community of selves—friends, family, fellow-workers—each interpreting themselves to one another. Obsessed with the problem of evil, Royce translated Christian notions of sin and forgiveness into communal terms, holding out for the ultimate overcoming of self-centeredness, alienation, and evil through loyalty in the Great or Beloved Community. Principal works: *The Spirit of Modern Philosophy, The World and the Individual, The Philosophy of Loyalty, Lectures on Modern Idealism.*

Edmund Husserl (1859–1938), German founder of the phenomenological movement, made the field of conscious intentions, considered in themselves apart from any questions about the reality of their objects, the subject of extensive investigations. He emphasized the pure description of whatever object or act would appear to or manifest in the field of consciousness, for instance, a work of art, a number, a judgment, an imagination. His methods and descriptions have been applied to the foundations of logic, to psychology and the social sciences, and to the analysis of literary texts and art. Principal works: *Logical Investigations, Ideas, Lectures on Internal Time-Consciousness, Transcendental Phenomenology, Cartesian Meditations.*

Henri Bergson (1859–1941) was a popular French thinker often described as a "process philosopher." Bergson stressed the importance of evolutionary change that is carried forth by a creative force (*elan vital*). He rejected the extremes of dualism and materialism, urging that an adequate metaphysics must account for our experience of a continuous, flowing time and must avoid the pitfalls of a mechanistic or "clock" time composed of distinct moments. In epistemology he stressed the importance of intuition and the limitations of intellectual knowledge. He influenced a generation of writers, including James Joyce. Principal works: *Time and Free Will, Creative Evolution, The Creative Mind, The Two Sources of Morality and Religion.*

John Dewey (1859–1952) was an American psychologist, philosopher, educator, and general defender of pragmatism in a wide range of contexts. He stressed that the primary purpose of philosophy should be to solve the problems of democratic society by the use of (a broader and more flexible version of) scientific method. Like Peirce, he advocated fallibilism, and he defended democracy on the grounds that it provides the best possible conditions for correcting our mistakes and solving common human problems. In education he stressed the importance of learning intellectual and practical skills in preference merely to memorizing facts. Principal works: *Logic: The Theory of Inquiry, The Quest for Certainty, Human Nature and Conduct, An Introduction to Social Psychology, Experience and Nature.*

Alfred North Whitehead (1861–1947), British mathematician, philosopher, and historian of ideas, is widely regarded as one of the great speculative metaphysicians and as the chief proponent of process philosophy. Whitehead stressed a universe in which change, creativity, and interdependence are reflected in immediate experience. Process is a creative advance in which all events ("actual occasions") emerge, evolve, and die through absorption in their offspring. Ordered change is possible through the interaction with a realm of eternal objects (similar to Platonic forms). God affects the world and is affected by it. Principal works: *Science and the Modern World, Process and Reality, Adventures of Ideas, Modes of Thought,* (with Bertrand Russell) *Principia Mathematica.*

Bertrand Russell (1872–1970), British logician, philosopher, and social critic, was one of the intellectual giants of the century. He developed, with Whitehead, a revolutionary system of symbolic logic, and he argued that logic is both the basis of mathematics and the proper method of philosophy. His theory of descriptions and denoting is a paradigm of logical analysis that shows how philosophers may be led by logical errors into incorrect metaphysical views, and his own metaphysics of logical atomism was derived from his logical system. In epistemology he is well known for his defense of empiricism, his distinction between knowledge by acquaintance and knowledge by description, and his claim that physical objects are logical constructions out of sense data. His criticism of religion and his liberal views on sex and marriage, socialism, and nuclear disarmament won him great admiration in some quarters but condemnation and censure in many others. Selected principal works: (with Whitehead) *Principia Mathematica*, "On Denoting," *The Problems of Philosophy*, *Our Knowledge of the External World*, *A History of Western Philosophy*, *Marriage and Morals*, *Principles of Social Reconstruction*, *Why I Am Not a Christian*.

George Edward Moore (1873–1958) was a British philosopher who taught at Cambridge during the early part of the twentieth century and who repudiated the neo-Hegelian idealism popular at the time and replaced it with a realistic philosophy of common sense. He claimed that commonsense propositions about time, space, material objects, and persons are known with certainty to be true. In emphasizing that the philosopher's task is that of analyzing the meanings of these propositions, Moore became one of the early proponents of linguistic analysis. He developed an intuitionist account of the nature of goodness and criticized earlier theories for committing the naturalistic fallacy—that is, the improper attempt to define "goodness" in terms of natural or metaphysical properties. Principal works: *Principia Ethica*, *Ethics*, *Philosophical Studies*, *Philosophical Papers*.

Karl Jaspers (1883–1969), a German existentialist who turned from medicine to philosophy, held that humans ideally seek transcendence, to "go beyond" themselves and a placid daily routine. Much of his work describes the boundaries of self-transcendence, which he identified as death, suffering, struggle/love, and guilt. They serve as the source of the main themes of much human communication and interaction, such as found in literature. They are a source of meaningfulness. Where self-transcendence fails on a large scale, we find irrational trends or mass movements, such as totalitarianism. Principal works: *Reason and Existenz*, *The Nature of Psychotherapy*, *Reason and Anti-Reason in Our Time*.

Ludwig Wittgenstein (1889–1951) was an Austrian who studied and taught in England and who greatly influenced twentieth-century analytic and linguistic philosophy. His early thought was concerned with the foundations of mathematics and the nature of linguistic representation. He developed a picture theory of language and sharply distinguished between what may properly be said—the realm of science—and what may only be shown—the realm of the mystical. He strongly influenced the logical positivists with his views that mathematical statements are tautologies and that metaphysical theories violate the limits of meaningful speech. His later thought in many ways repudiated his own earlier ideas. He came to emphasize that meaning is use within a language-game, that words do not acquire meaning by designating universal essences but rather may be applied on the basis of loose family resemblances, and that there can be no private language that refers to publicly inaccessible, inner events of the mind. These views, along with his conception of philosophy as an activity of describing ordinary use and removing conceptual confusion, are largely responsible for the rise of ordinary language philosophy. Principal works: *Tractatus Logico-Philosophicus, Philosophical Investigations.*

Gabriel Marcel (1889–1973) was a French phenomenologist and existentialist who held that the task of philosophy is to describe what it means to be in a concrete situation, avoiding at all costs abstractions, stereotypes, and statistical norms. Marcel held that human existence holds a number of clues or references to the "mystery of being" (the whole reality), which nonetheless cannot be encompassed by any thought systems. Some of these clues are the human body, having versus being, commitment, participation versus spectatorship, belonging, creative fidelity, and the encounter of others as persons, not objects. Principal works: *Metaphysical Journal, The Mystery of Being, The Philosophy of Existentialism.*

Martin Heidegger (1889–1976) was a German phenomenologist who developed and stressed many themes of existentialism. He held that man is a "being-in-the-world," that through our participation and involvement in it, the world constitutes our being. Our existence is characterized by three basic features: facticity (our involvement in the world), existentiality (an ongoing project embracing the tension between what we were and what we can become), and fallenness (the tendency to merely survive and not realize our potential). Through anxiety we encounter nothingness and finitude, but through freedom and the need to choose we can progress to an authentic existence. Heidegger has been influential in psychology. Principal works: *Being and Time, What Is Metaphysics?*

Gilbert Ryle (1900–1973), a British linguistic philosopher widely known for his attack on the Cartesian dualistic account of mind, claimed that the Cartesian theory postulates a mysterious and mythological "ghost in the machine," and he diagnosed the theory as being the result of a category mistake, a linguistic confusion whereby the categories of speech appropriate to physical objects and processes are used to talk about immaterial events in the ghostly mind. He went on to argue that ordinary talk about the mind really consists of statements about behavior and behavioral dispositions. Principal work: *The Concept of Mind.*

Jean-Paul Sartre (1905–1980) was a French philosopher who worked in the resistance during the Nazi occupation and is known for his popularization of existentialism via philosophical works, plays, novels, and short stories. He denied any "nature" of man preexisting individual choice. Individuals create their own natures through their free choices and actions; "existence comes before essence." He showed how people try to hide from themselves their freedom and responsibility by espousing determinism or essentialist theories like anti-Semitism or by engaging in other forms of self-deception (bad faith). Though he recognized the problems individuals in bad faith pose for one another—"Hell is other people"—he later focused on the way that man-made structures such as institutions can seriously restrict and undermine freedom. Principal works: *Being and Nothingness, Existentialism and Human Emotions, No Exit, Nausea, Critique of Dialectical Reason.*

Willard Quine (1908–2000), American logician and analytic philosopher, is influential for his criticisms of any hard-and-fast distinction between analytic and synthetic propositions and for his defense of the conventional nature of truth and the relativity of ontological commitment. The question of whether certain entities, such as minds, numbers, or even physical objects, "really exist" is, for Quine, a question about how propositions about those entities function in our language and what, if any, predictions they generate in the sciences. Principal works: *Methods of Logic, From a Logical Point of View, Word and Object, Ontological Relativity.*

Simone de Beauvoir (1908–1986), French existentialist, novelist, and feminist, is perhaps most widely known for her analysis of the ways women have been systematically cast in the role of "the other" and of the harmful effects of the way girls are often brought up. She stresses the ways society and its structures and institutions can inhibit an individual's self-consciousness and freedom. And she condemns as immoral those who try to hide their freedom from themselves or who refuse to act in accordance with their freedom and the freedom of others. Her novels explore themes such as human finitude, facing death, and the necessity of choice. Principal works: *The Second Sex, The Ethics of Ambiguity, Memoirs of a Dutiful Daughter, The Prime of Life.*

Alfred J. Ayer (1910–1991) was a British philosopher who brought to the English-speaking world the ideas of the logical positivists who were members of the Vienna Circle in Austria during the 1920s and 1930s. His very influential book *Language, Truth and Logic* became a popular manifesto of the logical positivist movement. In it he championed the verifiability principle, which requires that for a proposition to be meaningful it must be capable of empirical verification. He also maintained that mathematical statements are tautologies that tell us nothing about the world, that ethical utterances are no more than expressions of emotions, and that religious and metaphysical statements are nonsensical expressions empty of all cognitive content—themes that he later abandoned or qualified. Other principal works: *The Foundation of Empirical Knowledge, The Problem of Knowledge, The Concept of a Person.*

Albert Camus (1913–1960), French Algerian existential philosopher, journalist, and novelist, was convinced that the universe is benignly indifferent to human concerns and values. He argued that it is important to maintain this confrontation between the meaningless universe and the unsatisfied human demand for meaning. To this confrontation he gave the name "the absurd," and he challenged any activity other than rebellion or revolt that fails to keep the absurd "alive." He thus rejected suicide as well as leaps of faith that postulate the existence of meaning where there is none. He worked in the resistance during the Nazi occupation of France. Principal works: *The Myth of Sisyphus; The Rebel; Resistance, Rebellion and Death; The Stranger; The Plague; The Fall.*

Michel Foucault (1926–1984), French postmodern philosopher and historian of ideas, perhaps most widely known for his analyses of relations of power (with particular reference to human sexuality) and the historical relativity of knowledge. Power is everywhere, according to Foucault—as much between doctor and patient as between government and citizenry. His voluminous writings address three over-arching themes: (1) How do we understand ourselves as knowers? (2) How are people subjected in power relations? (3) How do we establish ourselves as moral agents? Any attempt to answer these questions in an absolute transhistorical fashion, independent of the cultural milieu of those who ask them, he argued, is doomed. True freedom is found only by questioning one's cherished assumptions and adopting perpetual openness toward the future. Principal works: *Madness and Civilization, The Order of Things, The Archeology of Knowledge, The History of Sexuality and Ethics: Subjectivity and Truth.*

Glossary

Following are definitions of terms likely to be encountered in beginning philosophy courses. They are not intended to be comprehensive or technically adequate in every respect. Words that appear in boldface letters in the definitions are themselves defined elsewhere in the Glossary.

A Posteriori Something known based upon experience.

A Priori Something known by reason, independent of experience.

Absolute (Objective) Idealism The view that reality is a single, ultimate, and all-encompassing spirit (the Absolute). According to Hegel, all change (biological, historical, or whatever) reflects cosmic spiritual evolution according to the principle that any limited or finite truth or thing may be viewed as a *thesis,* which in turn gives rise to an opposite, the *antithesis;* both are then synthesized in a larger whole. Usually involves a coherence theory of truth and a view of reality as manifesting itself in degrees or levels.

Ad Hoc "To this purpose," an explanation for an event or state of affairs, invented after the fact and for which there is no additional evidence.

Agnosticism In religion, the view that we cannot know or have no good reason for believing either that God exists or that He does not exist. Recommends suspension of belief.

Altruism As a moral thesis, altruism holds that we ought at least sometimes to put the interests of other persons ahead of our own. As a psychological thesis (contrasted with **psychological egoism**), it holds that we can put others' interests ahead of our own.

Analytic Statement A statement that is necessarily true by virtue of the meanings of its terms. Example: "If John is a capitalist, he can't be a Marxist." The denial of an analytic statement results in a **contradiction.** Analytic statements are sometimes said to give no new information about the world. Contrasted with **synthetic statements.**

Anarchism In political philosophy, the view that society ought to be without laws, rules, or governmental authority of any kind—that government is not a necessary condition of social order. Sometimes seen as a necessary stage in the transition toward better times or a new order.

Aristocracy Originally the term referred to a government controlled by those best suited to rule (for example, the wisest), but it has come to refer to a ruling class whose members were born into positions of power and wealth.

Atheism Strictly speaking, an atheist is one who denies the truth of **theism** in particular, but the term normally refers to any person who denies that a supreme being in any form exists.

Authenticity A term given special significance in existentialist thought, particularly that of Sartre. Roughly, it means choosing freely without rationalizing or pretending that someone or something made you choose the way you did and fully accepting the consequences of your choices. Often contrasted with an inauthentic act or lifestyle, examples of which are most easily found in Sartre's work. Thus, "It's expected of me" would be a paradigm case of inauthenticity.

Behaviorism In psychology, the view that nonphysical states of mind either do not exist or, if they do, are irrelevant to the proper goal of experimental psychology, namely, the prediction and control of behavior in terms of publicly observable variables (Skinner). In philosophy, the general view that mental terms, such as 'pain', 'emotion', or 'intelligence', can be expressed in a language involving only behavioral or physical states and dispositions of a person. Thus, according to Ryle, we can avoid the temptation to think of intelligence as a purely inner, spiritual faculty or process by seeing that the sentence "John is intelligent" is just a shorthand way of saying that in certain situations John is disposed to behave in ways we describe as "intelligent."

Brahman-Atman In Hindu religion and Vedantic philosophy Brahman is the universal, impersonal consciousness in which all things are sustained, that which transcends opposites (such as good and evil) and normal categories of understanding. *Atman* is the individual consciousness in each of us. Because of our ignorance (**maya**), we fail to realize that Atman is identical with Brahman. The goal of life is to experience this oneness with Brahman, thereby achieving liberation, joy, and peace (Shankara).

Causality (Entailment Theory) The view according to which two events are causally related if, given one, the second must follow; the second event is entailed by the first (the cause) even as a conclusion of a valid deductive argument is logically entailed by its premises (Ewing).

Causality (Regularity Theory) The view according to which two events are said to be causally related if they are constantly conjoined in space and time, that is, if one regularly follows the other. Nevertheless, no event necessitates or produces its particular effect. There is no necessity in nature, or if there is, we cannot know it. Thus, fire does not literally bring about heat but is statistically correlated with it, and the correlation enables us to formulate general laws (Hume).

Cogito Ergo Sum "I think, therefore I am" (Descartes).

Coherence Theory of Truth The view that a statement is true to the extent that it fits into a comprehensive network of logically related statements; that is, the statement follows from or entails other statements. Such a network is illustrated by the interlocking conceptions of mass, force, and velocity in physics. The coherence theory of truth is often associated with some form of **absolute (objective) idealism** (Blanshard).

Collectivism The view that in a political system the interests and moral–legal authority of the group should take precedence over the immediate interests of the individual. Personal interest in the long run is held to be best served by the system of which one is a part. Thus, Communism is a form of collectivism. Usually contrasted with individualism (as defended by Ayn Rand, for example).

Commonsense (Naive) Realism The view that our perceptual experience corresponds in all essential ways to the way the world in fact exists. With the exception of certain special cases, such as hallucinations, we directly perceive (the surface of) physical objects themselves (Moore).

Connotation The meaning of a term or phrase, usually expressed as the properties something must have in order to belong to a certain class. For example, being a closed, three-sided figure is part of the connotation of 'triangle', for something must possess these properties in order to be a triangle. Normally contrasted with **denotation.**

Contingent In a metaphysical or existential sense, something is contingent if it is subject to change (for instance, to birth and decay) or is dependent upon the existence of something else for its own existence. In logic, a proposition or sentence is contingent if it is not necessarily true or false; that is, its denial does not involve a contradiction (because its truth or falsity is determined by experience).

Contradiction A contradiction results when some belief or proposition is, directly or indirectly, both affirmed and denied to be the case in the same respect. Thus "It's raining, but it's not raining" is a direct contradiction, and "That's a square, but it has five sides" is an indirect contradiction. Note that "Jones is a cheapskate, but he regularly contributes to church" is not a contradiction because the same thing is not being both asserted and denied.

Correspondence Theory of Truth The view that statements are true if they correspond to facts or states of affairs in the world. Thus "Fido is on the mat" is true if Fido is in fact on the mat. Often associated with empiricist theories of knowledge (Russell).

Cosmological Argument An argument that attempts to demonstrate the existence of a divine being (God) by showing that there must be a "first cause" that brought the universe into being. The universe is said to exist contingently and to presuppose the existence of a necessary being who is uncaused and eternal. There are several important variations of the argument (Aquinas).

Cultural Relativism An empirical thesis that moral standards vary from one culture or group to another. There are no universally shared moral standards.

Deconstructionism A later twentieth-century literary and philosophical perspective that severely questions: (1) the objectivity of reason; (2) the ideal of a reality "out there" that we discover, rather than create; (3) the assumption of fixed foundations upon which all knowledge rests; (4) the goal of finding transcultural unity or universal essences in otherwise diverse human institutions and activities. Deconstructionism has no positive world view of its own. Rather, it is a semi-skeptical attitude that specializes in reducing philosophical theories to their psychological and linguistic roots.

Deduction In logic, the process of inferring a conclusion from one or more premises so that, if the inference is valid, the conclusion necessarily follows. Normally contrasted with **induction.**

Deism The belief that a supreme being created the universe, giving it natural laws to run itself, but that this being has henceforth not been involved in the affairs of humans (in establishing religion, for example).

Denotation That meaning of a term or phrase which is derived from the things or kinds of things to which the term refers. For example, 'philosopher' refers to (or denotes) the class of philosophers, which includes Socrates, Plato, Aristotle, and so on. This class is the denotation of the term. Normally contrasted with **connotation.**

Deontological Ethics Any ethical system or standard in which the rightness of an act is defined by reference to factors other than the act's consequences. For example, rightness may be determined by the motive of good will (Kant). Deontological ethicists are primarily concerned with issues of fairness, justice, and obligation rather than with personal happiness or social welfare. Normally contrasted with **teleological ethics.**

Deus ex Machina Sometimes rendered as the "ghost in the machine," it refers to a supernatural or magical entity postulated to account for some religious, scientific, or philosophical state of affairs.

Dialectical Materialism The metaphysical world view of Marxist-Leninist thought: Change is fundamental and occurs when conflicting material forces interact. Ideally, it results in a final state of perfection—the communist society. Economic struggle between classes is but one part of the larger evolutionary process.

Ding-an-Sich The "thing in itself," the reality behind its sensible appearances.

Dualism (Mind-Body) The view that the body and mind are two types of things, one physical, the other immaterial or spiritual. The most prominent version, interactionism, holds that each causes changes in the other (Descartes). Other versions, such as **epiphenomenalism,** have also been defended. A restricted contemporary version defends the dualism of mental and physical states but denies that the mind is a separate "thing," the possessor of mental states. Contrasted with **materialism.**

Efficient Cause According to Aristotle, the prior act or change (usually motion) that brings about some further change. Thus, hitting a person over the head is the efficient cause of that person's falling over. In science this is normally understood to be the only type of cause.

Emotivism The view that moral judgments, such as "Murder is wrong," are neither true nor false but are instead without cognitive meaning. Such judgments are merely expressions of feelings or attitudes and may involve the attempt to induce similar attitudes in others.

Empiricism The view according to which all knowledge, with the exception of mathematics and logic, is based upon and cannot go beyond what is known by experience. For example, since God presumably cannot be known by experience, an empiricist might attempt to explain different beliefs about God in terms of different psychological or cultural factors, which can be described and measured. Contrasted with **rationalism.**

Epiphenomenalism A dualistic theory of mind according to which molecular or neural changes in the brain are said to cause or "give off" distinctly mental effects, such as sensations or thoughts, which in themselves have no power to affect our physical states or behavior. Thus, the sensation of pain may be caused by a blow on the head, but the pain itself cannot cause my reaching for the aspirin; my physical reaction is caused by neural changes in the brain.

Esse Est Percipi "To be is to be perceived" (Berkeley).

Ethical Absolutism The view that there is at least one moral standard or rule (for example, the golden rule) binding on all persons. Contrasted with **ethical relativism.**

Ethical Egoism The view that rational or enlightened self-interest is the standard for judging the moral rightness or wrongness of actions. Thus, one ought to perform only those acts that maximize one's own good when there exists a choice. Not to be confused with **hedonism.**

Ethical Relativism The view that the moral rightness or wrongness of an act varies from culture to culture or, in an extreme form, from individual to individual. Thus, people from different cultures could disagree over the morality of an act and yet, from the perspective of their individual cultures, make a correct moral judgment.

Ex Nihilo Nihil Fit "From out of nothing, nothing comes."

Existentialism A general orientation in philosophy with no set of common principles. Among the themes stressed are the following: the importance of personal existence rather than abstract theorizing; the encounter with freedom and the necessity of choosing; the denial of any fixed human nature and of universal moral codes; the desirability of **authentic** lifestyles; and the encounter with death and meaninglessness (Sartre).

Fatalism The view that all events and human actions are eternally fixed and that trying to change the course of history is futile. On human actions fatalists therefore differ from hard determinists, who hold that personal effort and involvement can make a difference in the course of events, even though our efforts are themselves determined.

Feminism A philosophical orientation that stresses some combination of the following themes: greater economic, political, and social equality for women; the rejection of hierarchical power differentials; the achievements and abilities of women; the rejection of sexist language; and the identification and correction of (what may be) deep structural male bias in approaching questions of knowledge and reality.

Final Cause According to Aristotle, the end or purpose for which an object is brought into being or toward which it is developing. Associated with teleological explanations of behavior by reference to purposes or goals. Contrasted with **mechanism.**

Formal Cause According to Aristotle, that essence or intrinsic nature of something—its form—which manifests itself in a distinctive structure or pattern of organization. Thus, an acorn contains within itself the form of an oak tree.

Freedom The two most important senses from a philosophical point of view appear to be these: (1) the extent to which there are no restrictions, such as money, physical ability, social status, on what one desires to do; (2) not being totally subject to causal conditioning factors, having the ability, if a given situation were repeated, to choose a new course of action even if all the prior causes were the same. The former sense is usually associated with **soft determinism** and **liberalism,** the latter with **libertarianism** and indeterminism.

Hard Determinism The view that all events are 100 percent predictable in principle and are the necessary and inevitable results of prior causes. Any choice one may have made was strictly determined. It is impossible for any person ever to have chosen otherwise; hence no person is morally responsible for his or her actions. Differs from **soft determinism** in assuming an incompatibility between freedom and causation and in denying both freedom and moral responsibility.

Hedonism As a theory of human nature, psychological hedonism stresses that persons innately seek, as ends in themselves, to experience pleasure and to avoid pain. An *ethical* hedonist holds that pleasure is the only thing that is intrinsically desirable or "good" in itself (Epicurus). When combined with other assumptions, ethical hedonism furnishes a standard for judging the moral rightness or wrongness of actions. An example of such a combination is the **utilitarianism** of Jeremy Bentham.

Holism In science and philosophy, the view that the properties and behavior of "whole" systems or objects (cells, persons, societies, etc.) cannot be reduced to, or explained fully by reference to, the properties and behavior of their parts. Holists typically stress the interdependence of different levels of explanation. (Contrasted with **reductionism** or **materialism.**)

Humanism The view that human nature and experience, rather than, say, God's will or social custom, ought to be the basis of our religious, moral, social, and political values and ideals. Humanism is often associated with self-realizationist philosophies and psychologies (Erich Fromm).

Idealism The general view that matter is reducible to mind or has no existence apart from mind and that reality consists of only mental entities, such as consciousness, thought, and experience. The two most important forms are Berkeley's **subjective idealism** and Hegel's **absolute idealism.**

Identity Theory A modern materialist theory of mind, which holds that although psychological and physical terms (such as "depression" and "C fibers firing") mean different things, they refer to the same brain processes, just as "water" and "H_2O" refer to the same substance. Depression is thus identical with the brain process (for example, "C fibers firing") with which it is correlated (J. C. Smart).

Induction The process of organizing the data from observation and experimentation to provide evidence in varying degrees of probability for a particular conclusion. Induction might be used in solving a crime, for example, or in supporting a scientific law. Inductive evidence never entails the conclusion as the premises of a valid deductive argument entail the conclusion.

Liberalism In its original or classical sense, a social-political theory that the rights and self-determination of individuals should be given precedence over external or governmental authority in all but the most basic areas. Recently, it has come to mean the opposite view, which stresses the authority and responsibility of government to improve its citizens' well-being.

Libertarianism The doctrine according to which persons can transcend their causal conditioning to choose between alternative actions (see **freedom**) and should be held morally responsible for their actions. Indeterminism, the view that free actions have no causes, is a special version of libertarianism. In political philosophy, the view that persons should be given maximum personal freedom from the intervention of other persons or government in their lives.

Logical Positivism A scientifically oriented philosophical school of the 1930s and 1940s that purported to eliminate much of philosophy and religion as meaningless by applying the criterion of verifiability and to restate and resolve the remaining issues in a rigorous formal language. Thus, "God exists" and "God does not exist" are equally meaningless because they are unverifiable.

Marxism A loose-knit theory, with important variations, of scientific socialism based on the economic, political, and social principles of Karl Marx. Among its chief tenets or concerns are these: the struggle between classes, the labor theory of value, the nature of alienation, the call for revolutionary action, and historical materialism. See also **Dialectical Materialism.**

Material Cause According to Aristotle, the stuff of which something is made and which persists through time despite changes in its empirical properties.

Materialism That view of reality according to which matter, whatever it may turn out to be (for example, atoms, mass and energy, electrons), is the basis of all that is—the stuff of the universe. Mental or spiritual entities, such as mind or God, are either rejected or reduced to matter. See also **Reductionism.**

Maya A concept in Hindu or Vedantic thought, sometimes translated as "illusion." The doctrine of maya does not deny the existence of the sensory world, but rather it denies that this world of independent material objects is ultimately real. See also **Brahman-Atman** (Shankara).

Mechanism The view that certain (perhaps all) phenomena can be explained by material bodies, their position and motion, and the forces that act upon them. Thus, Hobbes's explanation of desire as the motion of tiny particles in one's head toward the object of desire was essentially mechanistic. Closely related to **materialism.**

Metaethics The study of the meanings of moral terms such as 'good', 'right', and 'duty' and of the logical processes involved in moral arguments and decision making. In metaethics one seeks to understand moral language rather than to decide how persons ought to behave in moral situations (the province of **normative** ethics). **Emotivism,** for example, is a metaethical position which denies that moral judgments have any fact-stating function.

Monism Quantitative monism is the view that reality is "one," an integrated whole in which all seemingly separate things are sustained and united. That persons are parts of a "group mind" is one type of monistic thesis. Contrasted with quantitative **pluralism.** *Qualitative* monism is the view that reality consists of only one type of thing. For example, in the **materialist** view reality consists of matter; in the **idealist** view, of ideas. Contrasted with qualitative **pluralism** and **dualism.**

Mysticism A metaphysical and religious world view largely based on the claims of some persons to have experienced a oneness with God, a universal consciousness, or possibly even nature itself. Tending toward **monism** or **pantheism,** it often includes the claim that the individual "I" or ego and the appearance of distinct objects are illusions and reflect our ignorance of the basic unity of all things (Buddha). Cloudy thinking, intuition, or occult studies should not be confused with mysticism as it is defined here.

Natural Law A regulative principle, such as the ideal of justice or the tendency of persons to "aim for the good," which exists in nature independently of legislation or convention. Natural laws are assumed not to change, although our conceptions of them may change. In legal philosophy, they are contrasted with *positive* (man-made) laws. They may or may not be seen as decreed by God. They are knowable by reason and exhibit a prescriptive or guiding force in their respective domains as in, for example, the domain of physical processes or the development of moral or legal codes.

Naturalism In metaphysics and epistemology, the view that the natural world or universe as known by experience is reality. Naturalism is usually broadly based and less **reductionist** than **materialism.** In ethics, the view that moral judgments may be known to be true or false by applying empirical standards such as personal feelings, human nature, or evolution. For example, judgment X is wrong because it does not contribute to self-realization.

Necessary and Sufficient Conditions Something is a necessary condition if it must be the case in order for something else to be the case. Something is a sufficient condition if, given that condition, something else necessarily follows or must become the case.

New Age Philosophy A loose-knit convergence of ideas typically stressing the legitimacy of paranormal experiences, reincarnation, and spiritual evolution; alternative medical practices (homeopathy, visualization, etc.); acceptance of responsibility for what we create or attract; peace, environmental protection, and respect ("the Earth is our Mother"); and mutual empowerment in preference to competition and hierarchical social structures.

Nihilism In metaphysics, the view that nothing that seems to exist is real. In moral, political, and social thought, the view that there is no objective basis for shared values and that, strictly speaking, life is valueless or meaningless.

Normative Pertaining to a standard or rule for guiding behavior; a regulative principle as may be found, for example, in ethics, religion, or politics. Normative ethics is the study of fundamental moral standards such as embodied by hedonism, egoism, the golden rule, and so forth. Whenever one asks "What *ought* to be the case?" as opposed to "What *is* the case?" one is asking a normative question.

Ontological Argument An argument, first put forth by Saint Anselm, that since perfection entails existence, we can deduce the existence of God from our concept of Him as a perfect being.

Panentheism The view that a divine being is both transcendent and immanent in all things. The physical universe is but one aspect of a transcendent reality. In Hinduism, this distinction is reflected in the difference between Higher (impersonal) Brahman and Lower (personal) Brahman.

Pantheism The view that God or the divine is totally immanent in all things, not distinct from nature or the universe (Spinoza).

Phenomenology A twentieth-century philosophical movement, distinctive for its careful, unbiased method of describing the universal characteristics (meanings) of any object (phenomenon) that appears to consciousness, such as a logical rule, a value, a feeling, an idea, or a material object. Phenomenologists are antireductionist (Husserl). Some **existentialists** (Sartre) are also phenomenologists, but there are important differences between the two approaches to philosophy.

Platonism Any philosophy closely related to that of Plato in essential respects. Usually a view that emphasizes the reality of changeless forms of being and eternal truths over that of sense experience and the changing material world; the latter are interpreted as mere "appearances." An illustration of this view is so-called Platonic love, which stresses the ideal of lasting, categorical friendship in preference to the passions of the moment.

Pluralism *Quantitative* pluralism is the view that there is an indefinitely large number of basic entities (such as atoms) of which everything else is made. These entities may or may not be of a single kind or type. *Qualitative* pluralism is the view that there are at least two (possibly more) kinds or types of basic elements that make up the universe. Thus mind-body **dualism** is one type of qualitative pluralism.

Postmodernism A loosely knit affiliation of twentieth-century perspectives that includes **existentialism, deconstructionism, feminism,** and, by some accounts, **New Age** thought. Postmodernists generally question: (1) the objectivity of reason; (2) the ideal of a preexisting reality "out there" that we allegedly discover rather than in large part create through our interpretations; (3) the idea that there are relatively fixed foundations upon which all knowledge rests; (4) the goal of finding unity or universal essences in institutions, such as religion, or in categories such as 'women' or 'power', where there is instead great diversity or at best only certain "family resemblances." Postmodernists pay particular attention to those cultural institutions and influences, such as patriarchy, political power, technology, sexuality, or language itself, that shape and otherwise relativize our knowledge and expectations.

Pragmatism, Pragmatic Theory of Truth The view that the meaning of an idea is determined by reference to its scientific, personal, or social consequences. What difference would such and such an idea make if it were adopted? The pragmatic test of truth is whether an idea "successfully" guides us in a particular endeavor; 'success' here is interpreted in different ways, for example, as enhancing personal satisfaction (William James) or predictive power and fruitfulness in further inquiry (Charles Peirce). Pragmatists generally tend toward **naturalism** in metaphysics and anti**rationalism** in epistemology.

Primary and Secondary Qualities An epistemological and metaphysical distinction widely held by philosophers and physicists of the sixteenth and seventeenth centuries. A primary quality is one that is part of the nature of material objects in the external world; size, shape, and motion are primary qualities. A secondary quality is a certain "power" material objects have to produce secondary ideas (perceptions) in us; thus, color, temperature, odor, and sound are not in the objects themselves but are instead in our minds (Locke).

Process Philosophy An orientation rooted principally in the thought of Alfred North Whitehead, Henri Bergson, and Charles Hartshorne (and to some extent the pragmatists Peirce, James, and Dewey). It stresses the relative and evolutionary character of conceptual frameworks, the existence of novelty and creative advance in nature, the denial of inert substances and fixed essences, and a naturalistic approach to questions of value. *Process theology* stresses both God and humankind as cocreators in a grand, though not predictable, evolutionary scheme.

Psychological Egoism The view that persons are by nature selfish and incapable of ever putting the interests of others ahead of their own. Often cited as a basis for **ethical egoism.** Contrasted with **altruism** (Hobbes).

Raison d'Etre "Reason for being," the rationale for, or point of, the existence of something.

Rationalism A pervasive orientation (with many variations) in metaphysics and epistemology, the view that reason is the fundamental means of knowing reality. It stresses necessarily true propositions, a method of strict deduction, the quest for absolute certainty in knowledge, and the irrelevance or deceptive nature of sensory experience. For most rationalists the world is not in reality as it appears to common sense. Contrasted with **empiricism** (Plato, Descartes).

Reductio ad Absurdum An argument that leads to a consequence that contradicts one or more assumptions of the argument. Hence, the argument reduces to absurdity because it leads to a contradiction.

Reductionism *Explanatory* reductionism holds that the laws and theories at one level of inquiry (such as psychology) can in principle be translated into or accounted for by laws and theories at a more fundamental level of inquiry (such as biochemistry); the ideal is to provide one unified set of explanations for all natural phenomena. *Metaphysical* reductionism holds that the entities or processes at one level (for example, such psychological states as depression) are nothing more than entities or processes at a more fundamental level (for example, the firing of neurons).

Representative Realism (Causal Theory of Perception) The view that our perceptions are caused by external objects that are either partly or wholly unlike the perceptions they cause. The world is in fact rather different from the way we perceive it, as is evidenced, for example, in Eddington's description of two tables in Chapter I. Sometimes closely associated with the distinction between **primary and secondary qualities** (Russell, Locke).

Scholasticism A philosophical orientation closely allied with Christian theology and usually taken to have emerged in the ninth century, although its roots go back to early Christian thought and to Saint Augustine. Scholastics dealt extensively with such issues as the problem of universals, the relation between faith and reason, and the existence and nature of God. They developed extensive technical philosophical vocabularies, drew important and sometimes fine distinctions, and developed tightly reasoned arguments that relied heavily on syllogistic logic. Boethius, Saint Anselm, and Saint Thomas Aquinas (the founder of modern day Thomism), for example, were Scholastics.

Skepticism In ordinary usage the view that little should be taken for granted and that even beliefs widely held should be subjected to critical analysis. A skeptic in this sense would not necessarily assume that "Progress is good." In philosophical discussion, skepticism expresses the attitude that our beliefs can never be rationally certain or, in extreme forms, that it is impossible ever to know anything.

Social Contract The thesis that government is made possible by a "contract" between individuals who give up certain rights to a central authority, such as a monarch, in return for the promise of a peaceful and orderly life wherein other rights may be enjoyed. There are substantial variations on this general view, depending, for example, on whether the central authority is itself believed to be a party to the contract (Locke, Hobbes).

Soft Determinism The view that although all actions are caused, not all are compelled. Free (uncompelled) acts are those that follow from the desires of the agent. Whether or not human behavior turns out to be completely predictable, there is thus a place for both freedom and morally responsible action.

Solipsism A metaphysical solipsist holds that nothing outside of his own consciousness and experience actually exists; life is analogous to a "dream." An epistemological solipsist holds that he has direct or certain knowledge of only his own experience and that his beliefs about an external world of other persons and material objects are at best only problematic inferences based upon his experience and cannot be known to be true.

Stoicism The view that the virtuous life is one that conforms to nature and reflects both peace of mind and equal indifference to good fortune or disaster. Everything in the Stoic's world has its rational place and is as it should be. Strong emphasis is placed on rational self-discipline (Marcus Aurelius).

Sub Specie Eternitatis "From the perspective of eternity," for example, from God's point of view.

Subjective Idealism The view that the objects of perception are not material substances but are instead "ideas" or collections of sensations that could not exist apart from their being perceived by some mind. **Esse est percipi,** "To be is to be perceived" (Berkeley).

Subjectivism In epistemology, the view that what we know is always conditioned by, or must be judged in relation to, individual consciousness. A radical version is **subjective idealism.** In ethics, the view that good and evil are the objects of positive and negative attitudes respectively; judgments of right and wrong basically reflect personal preference. "Man is the measure of all things" (Protagoras).

Substance Something is a substance in one or more of the following senses (first noted by Aristotle): a concrete, particular thing (tree) seen as the unity of form or structure and material stuff; a substratum that supports empirical properties, the stuff remaining when all characteristics are subtracted; a center of change retaining its numerical identity through time despite a change in its empirical characteristics; an entity existing in its own right, not directly dependent on something else for its existence as are, for example, properties and relations. The last three senses tended to be emphasized by modern philosophers, such as Descartes and Locke.

Summum Bonum The "supreme good" or ultimate happiness.

Synthetic Statement Any statement whose denial is not self-contradictory. Also said to be informative, that is, to convey factual data about the world. May be **a priori** or **a posteriori,** although this continues to be debated. Contrasted with **analytic statements.**

Tautology Any statement that is necessarily true by virtue of its truth-functional parts; one that involves a fundamental law of logic. Example: "It is either raining or it is not." Tautologies are usually said to be empty of content, that is, to lack information.

Teleological Argument An argument that attempts to demonstrate the existence of a divine being by pointing to the existence of order, purpose, and (alleged) intelligent design in the universe (William Paley).

Teleological Ethics Any ethical system that defines moral rightness or wrongness in terms of the goodness or badness of an action's consequences—for instance, how much pleasure or happiness results from the action. Hedonism, egoism, and utilitarianism are usually forms of teleological ethics. Sometimes described as consequentialism.

Teleology The view that purposes and goal-directedness are an intrinsic part of the universe, particularly in the case of living forms. Thus, teleological explanations in science attempt to explain some animal or human behavior by reference to the state or end apparently being sought after. A simple example: "Jones went to the beach in order to get a suntan."

Theism The view that there is but one perfect and supreme being who created the world, who is at least partly distinct from it, and who is (or ought to be) the object of religious worship.

Universal A common characteristic possessed by the members of a given class; the blueness of blue objects, the justice of just acts. A *realist* holds that universals exist independent of particular things (Plato). A *conceptualist* holds that they are concepts in the mind (Locke). A *nominalist* holds that they are words used to describe similarities in things; only particulars are real (Ockham).

Utilitarianism The moral standard that the right action, of those alternatives open to the agent, is one that produces the greatest possible good (pleasure or happiness) for the greatest number of people (John Stuart Mill). A special version, *rule* utilitarianism, holds that acts are right if they conform to certain moral rules (for example, "Always keep your promises") that are themselves justifiable because following them will in the long run result in the greatest overall well-being.

Validity A valid argument is a deductive argument in which the conclusion necessarily follows from the premises; one in which if the premises are true the conclusion must also be true. If the conclusion does not necessarily follow, the argument is invalid. Thus, "All men are mortal. Socrates is a man. Therefore, Socrates is mortal" is a valid argument. Validity is a function of logical form alone, and does not apply to inductive arguments or to simple sentences.

Verifiability Criterion of Meaning The position that, with the exception of the propositions of mathematics and logic (which are necessarily true by definition), a statement must in principle admit of some empirical evidence that would verify or falsify it, in order to be cognitively meaningful. See also **Logical Positivism.**

Weltanschauung "World view," or general outlook on life.

Index